The Beauty Within

The
Beauty
Within

ROSALYN DERGES

CWR

Copyright © Rosalyn Derges, 2019

Published 2019 by CWR, Waverley Abbey House, Waverley Lane, Farnham,
Surrey GU9 8EP, UK.

CWR is a Registered Charity – Number 294387 and a Limited Company registered in
England – Registration Number 1990308.

The right of Rosalyn Derges to be identified as the author of this work has been asserted
by her in accordance with the Copyright, Designs and Patents Act 1988.

For a list of National Distributors, visit cwr.org.uk/distributors

Scripture references are taken from the New Living Translation, Copyright © 1996, 2004,
2015 by Tyndale House Foundation.

Other versions are marked: *The Message*, Copyright © 1993, 1994, 1995, 1996, 2000,
2001, 2002 by Eugene H. Peterson; NIV: New International Version® Anglicised, NIV®
Copyright © 1979, 1984, 2011 by Biblica, Inc.®; AMPC: The Amplified Bible, Classic Edition,
Copyright © 1954, 1958, 1962, 1964, 1965, 1987 by the Lockman Foundation. GNB: Good
News Bible © 2004 published by The Bible Societies/Collins © American Bible Society.
All rights reserved.

Concept development, editing, design and production by CWR.

Every effort has been made to ensure that this book contains the correct permissions
and references, but if anything has been inadvertently overlooked the Publisher will be
pleased to make the necessary arrangements at the first opportunity. Please contact the
Publisher directly.

Printed in China by 1010 Printing

ISBN: 978-1-78259-832-9

Dedication

I would like to dedicate this book to all women who have a desire to grow in the likeness of Jesus and discover how beautiful they are. You are the beloved of God and can truly reflect something of His awesome character in your everyday lives. You are beautiful.

Contents

Thank you

The journey towards writing *The Beauty Within* has been accompanied with wonderful people who have encouraged me along the way. I would like to thank and acknowledge them for their tireless support as I grow and develop as a daughter of the King, and as a woman who longs to become all I am meant to be.

My wonderful husband Steve has been my greatest encourager. Steve, you have released me to pursue my dreams in order to learn, teach and share at CWR these past 18 years. Thank you for being a rock, and for always giving me a wonderful homecoming, with a gleaming house! Your commitment to serving God, your walk of faith, and your devotion to family is an inspiration.

Lucy and Michael, my two fabulous children. You were the desire of my heart before I knew you, and the most amazing gift of God. When you came into our lives you brought so much love, fun and joy. Your part in my journey has been of incredible significance. Thank you.

My terrific parents. Your love and belief in me has enabled me to pursue what I love to do. And Denise, my gorgeous sister, who constantly encourages and is someone with whom I can share at the deepest of levels.

Angie, my teacher, co-worker, mentor and friend. This part of my journey started with you building into my life with your own experiences. You have been an inspiration as a trainer and mentor who showed me how to train others in my own unique way. You taught me how to get in touch with my spontaneous side – well done!

My friend Miriam. Because of your devotion to the Word of God and how it has impacted your life, you have inspired me to develop a love for studying, and applying that precious Word to everyday life. Your friendship has been incredible over the many years we have known one another. You are truly a beautiful woman of God.

Lynette and Rosie, my dear companions in women's ministry. Thank you for the wonderful weekends of fun, friendship and teaching we have shared in this great ministry at CWR. The Beauty Within weekends were especially fabulous because of you both. Thank you Lynette, for giving me the opportunity to speak and write – I have loved every minute of it.

Andrea Bodle for editing and Joanna Duke for designing. You have brought to life what I had envisioned in my mind for this book, and made it even more wonderful than I could imagine. Thank you.

Tutors and staff at Waverley Abbey College. Without the counselling course I embarked on in 2001, I feel I would never have been in a position to teach, train and write in this way. You have given me both the training and the platform to fulfil the call on my life. Thank you.

None of this would have been possible without the love, encouragement and transforming power of my Father God, precious Lord Jesus and wonderful Holy Spirit. Your presence in my life has been the single most empowering and incredible part of this journey. You are truly amazing!

Before we begin...

S ome time ago, I was invited to speak at a women's weekend retreat. What joy! This is something I love to do, and I started to think about what would be helpful to share.

A few days later, while looking into my bathroom mirror, my flaws and imperfections seemed particularly noticeable. While my hair looked alright, I couldn't help but focus on the areas I didn't like such as the odd wrinkle or laughter line (at least those go up and not down!). And then it came to me – the beauty *within* was of significantly more value than the beauty *without*. Inspired, I started to jot down thoughts about the joy of discovering, developing and purposely pursuing our inner beauty – and the theme of the weekend was born. It was a wonderful time of becoming aware of our uniqueness and appreciating our God-given gifts.

At the close of the retreat, several women expressed an interest in the idea of continuing to explore this great topic in the form of a spiritual journey. And so here it is! An opportunity to take some time to discover what is going on inside our inner being. We will refer to our hearts, minds and spirits as we go along:

Our hearts hold our desires, intentions and emotions.

Our minds play a large part in affecting our behaviour as we think, in both positive and negative terms. We often refer to the heart and mind as the soul.

Our spirit is the place where we fully experience God as Spirit, and have a connection with Him, which flamed into being when Jesus came into our life. This part of us is what grows and matures as we become more aware of, and in tune with, what God is saying to us.

So every part of us, spirit, soul and body will be open to uncovering the truth about how God sees us. Looking up, looking in and looking out will help to refocus our inner being, and help us to evaluate where we are on our life journey.

As you work through this devotional journal, take time over each session. You might want to do one each day, or you may want to stay with one in particular for a longer period of time. Go at your own pace and let God by His Spirit speak into your spirit, mind and heart.

Our focus will be on personal growth and development, and there are three areas that we will be considering throughout:

• Our relationship with Father, Son and Holy Spirit – how we perceive them, what we know about them, and how that impacts our faith.
• How we perceive ourselves – what goes on in our thinking, how we view the world around us, and where we place our priorities.
• How we relate to those around us – with whom do we spend our time, and how do we live out our faith in terms of what we do and how we behave in the various activities we are involved in?

I pray that as we go on this journey together, you will be inspired by the Holy Spirit to understand who you are in Christ Jesus and how much you are loved by the Father. As you discover your inner beauty, may you also find contentment and peace, be a blessing to others and glorify God.

Journaling

'I will climb up to my watchtower and stand at
my guardpost. There I will wait to see what
the LORD says and how he will answer my
complaint. Then the LORD said to me, "Write
my answer plainly on tablets, so that a runner
can carry the correct message to others."'
Habakkuk 2:1–2

There are so many beautiful journals, bullet journals and
diaries available, in all shapes and sizes. It seems that
writing for one's own pleasure is still very popular. This
journal has been created with the intention that you will feel free
to write about what's on your mind as well as an opportunity
for God's Spirit to speak to you as you doodle, create and write.
Join me as we explore our theme of the beauty within while
journaling, drawing, creating, colouring and listening to what the
Lord wants to say to us.

In these verse, Habakkuk appears to wait before God with
an open heart and mind ready to 'see' what He will say. God
clearly wants him to write it down. We juggle and hold so
many things in our head; writing our thoughts down helps us to
remember and to clear that cluttered mind feeling. Later, when
we have more time, we can read over those precious thoughts
and give them our proper attention.

Reflect

Spend time in God's presence, first speaking to Him and then listening to Him. I once wrote a song with these words:

'Two-way conversation with my Lord. Two-way conversation word by word. Telling Him I love Him, telling me He loves me. Precious moments sharing; moments filled with love.'

As you reflect on, and colour in, the verse below, become aware of God's presence and consider what you might say to Him, and what He might say to you. Weave your own words in and around the verse.

'May the words of my mouth and the meditation of my heart be pleasing to you, O Lord, my rock and my redeemer.' Psalm 19:14

The journey begins!

'Jesus replied, "'You must love the LORD
your God with all your heart, all your soul,
and all your mind.' This is the first and
greatest commandment. A second is equally
important: 'Love your neighbour as yourself.'"'
Matthew 22:37–39

Writing things down or journaling has been linked to improved mental health and wellbeing. Our journey into journaling begins with these two thoughts: the importance of loving God, and loving others as yourself. Yes, that's right, we need to love *ourselves*! What we think, how we feel and the way we behave all stems from what is going on inside. So as we reflect, write and create our way through this journal, we can also begin to appreciate who we are and value our thoughts.

Have there been ways in which you have developed in character and relationships over the last few months? This could include times where you have encouraged and helped others in their own personal growth and development. Have you learned something new, achieved a goal or taken part in an event that has been a blessing to others? We can find it difficult to celebrate our achievements, can't we? Yet God celebrated His when He looked at what He had made and 'he saw that it was very good!' (Gen. 1:31).

Reflect and write

Write down five things you have accomplished or been involved in throughout the past year.

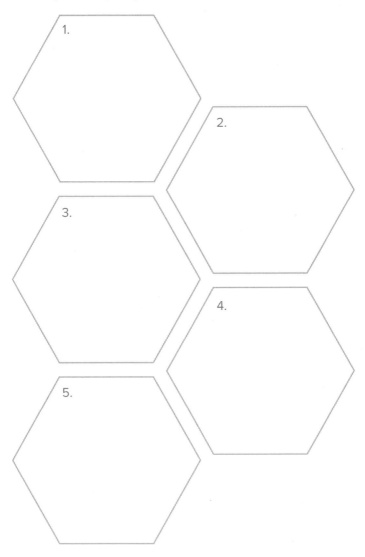

1.

2.

3.

4.

5.

Develop the beauty within

'You should clothe yourselves instead with the beauty that comes from within, the unfading beauty of a gentle and quiet spirit, which is so precious to God.' **1 Peter 3:4**

We live in a world where outer beauty is celebrated, and eternal youth seems to be desired. Magazines encourage us to look younger, thinner and fitter. We might even be tempted into considering surgery in order to roll back the years. There is nothing wrong with fashion and make-up. I myself enjoy thinking about what outfit to wear, and putting on make-up — it can be fun! But I am aware of the words in the verse above, which encourage us to focus on what we are like inside.

We may not described ourselves as having a 'gentle and quiet spirit' at present but there is something here that gives us hope that our inner selves can be developed. Peter tells us we should clothe ourselves with a different kind of beauty. *The Message* puts it this way: 'Cultivate inner beauty, the gentle, gracious kind that God delights in.' So we need to be proactive if we are to grow spiritually. God is inviting us to walk with Him as we pursue the kind of growth and development that has nothing to do with outward appearance but with a maturity within — the beauty within.

Reflect and write

What aspects of 'the beauty within' do you see in others that you admire? For example, someone who shows kindness and takes time to listen to others. Jot a few down here.

Having 'beauty within' is closely related to having inner peace or contentment. Proverbs 14:30 says: 'A calm and undisturbed mind and heart are the life and health of the body' (AMPC). This presents a picture of someone who is at peace, which in turn benefits their physical and spiritual life. Our sense of wellbeing can easily be affected by things that are going on in our daily lives such as discontentment with where we live, the tendency to compare ourselves to others, as well as the general busyness of life as we dash about trying to fit everything in.

Write

Consider three other things that can affect your 'inner contentment'.

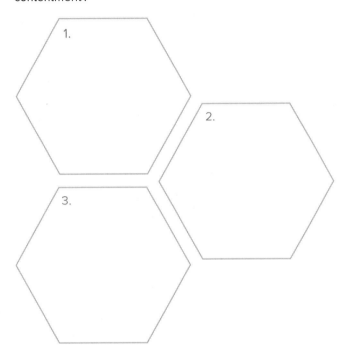

1.

2.

3.

Dear Lord, show me how to cultivate inner beauty with Your help and guidance. Help me to become aware of those things that would take away my peace, and work with You to clothe myself with the beauty that comes from You. Thank You that Your Word says, 'The LORD gives strength to his people; the LORD blesses his people with peace' (Psa. 29:11, NIV). Bless me with Your peace right now Lord, and give me the strength to live a life that delights You. Amen.

What's inside?

'I pray that your hearts will be flooded with light so that you can understand the confident hope he has given to those he has called—his holy people who are his rich and glorious inheritance.' **Ephesians 1:18**

Years ago, I would go with my parents to Blackpool for the dancing competitions, where they competed successfully in the events. Yes! I walked on that famous sprung floor, it was such a lot of fun! Part of those trips meant we got to enjoy Blackpool rock, which, of course, has 'Blackpool Rock' written all the way through it. Sometimes I wonder what would be written on the inside of me.

What is truly inside of us? What is written on our hearts, our minds and our spirits? Just as Russian nesting dolls have a set of decreasing dolls within, so we have elements such as fears, hopes, passions, disappointments, hurts, buried deep in our lives. Prayerfully, we can explore and discover how these deeper areas can influence us and our behaviour.

Reflect and write

Ask yourself these questions:

- What's on my mind – what do I find myself thinking?
- What's in my heart – what are my desires?
- What is my spiritual wellbeing like – how closely am I connected in my relationship with God?

Now write in the largest doll which area has the greatest priority in your life: mind, heart or spirit; the second largest doll, the second priority and so on:

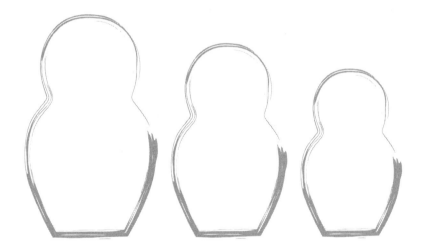

Which are you most likely to be led by?

....

We have to come to this with an honest attitude. The truth is we are not perfect; we make mistakes. We are not defined by what we do, where we live, who we know or how much money we have. The Bible says it is much deeper than that, as we can see in the verses below.

Reflect and write

Reflect on these verses. How do they bless your spirit, heart and mind? Jot down your thoughts on the next page.

'I pray that your hearts will be flooded with light so that you can understand the confident hope he has given to those he has called—his holy people who are his rich and glorious inheritance' (Eph. 1:18).

'O my people, trust in him at all times. Pour out your heart to him, for God is our refuge' (Psa. 62:8).

'Then you will experience God's peace, which exceeds anything we can understand. His peace will guard your hearts and minds as you live in Christ Jesus' (Phil. 4:7).

'Think about the things of heaven, not the things of earth' (Col. 3:2).

'All praise to God, the Father of our Lord Jesus Christ, who has blessed us with every spiritual blessing in the heavenly realms because we are united with Christ' (Eph. 1:3).

'Through him you Gentiles are also being made part of this dwelling where God lives by his Spirit' (Eph. 2:22).

Spirit

Heart

Mind

I am known

'O LORD, you have examined my heart and
know everything about me. You know when
I sit down or stand up. You know my thoughts
even when I'm far away. You see me when
I travel and when I rest at home. You know
everything I do. You know what I am going to
say even before I say it, LORD. You go before
me and follow me. You place your hand of
blessing on my head.' **Psalm 139:1–5**

When we moved to glorious Devon, it was a dream
come true. Walks by the sea taken in all weathers.
What a blessing! But along with the move came the
tedious change of address notifications including a new driving
licence with a photo identity card attached. For this, I had to
prove my identity with various documents.

My identity seemed to be tied up with my birth certificate or
passport, and perhaps a utility bill. It got me thinking: 'What
is my true identity?' I am more than a few documents; more
than my age and job experiences. I am more than what my
photograph portrays.

This psalm declares an amazing truth that God knows what goes
on in every part of my being. God knows me! And He knows

you too. He knows everything about each one of us intimately. Notice how the verses say that God knows about our hearts, when we sit or stand, our thoughts, when we travel or rest at home, everything we do and everything we say. It is reassuring to know that He cares so much about every area of our lives.

Write

Jot down below any words or phrases from Psalm 139:1–5 that leap out for you, and why they do.

....

....

....

....

....

....

....

....

Verse 5 says something wonderful: 'You go before me and follow me. You place your hand of blessing on my head.' God walks with us and blesses us. Walking before us, He shows us the way to go; walking behind us, He watches over us as we go along our path in life.

As we continue to reflect on our inner being, let's remember this biblical truth: *we are known.*

Reflect and write

God is with you in every part of your life. How does that make you feel? Which areas do you particularly need to sense His presence?

Say the words of Psalm 139:1–5 (aloud if possible) as a prayer. As you do, praise the Lord for His constant presence, and perhaps ask that you are particularly aware of His nearness in certain situations.

The Father notices

'What is the price of two sparrows—one copper coin? But not a single sparrow can fall to the ground without your Father knowing it. And the very hairs on your head are all numbered. So don't be afraid; you are more valuable to God than a flock of sparrows.' **Matthew 10:29–31**

One morning, walking along the coast at Budleigh Salterton in Devon, I was admiring the beautiful scenery of the pebbly beach, the magnificent red cliffs and the green hills around me. Seagulls were flying overhead and people were enjoying the sunshine. That day, I couldn't help but feel joy and a desire to rejoice – it was wonderful!

The creator envisioned everything I could see including tiny flowers hidden in the hedgerows, and the little creatures in the rock pools. As I took all this in, I was reminded of these verses where it tells us that God notices everything. Jesus encourages us not to be afraid because the Father values us significantly more than a flock of sparrows.

If you can, take a walk outside today, and pay particular attention to what you see and hear. Notice the small things as well as the bigger things. Look at people's faces and be aware that God loves each one of them. He created them too. If you aren't able to get out today, look around your home, place of work or simply out of a window. Try to become aware of your surroundings with a keen eye. We can so easily miss the little things because we are busy, or have become used to them.

Write

What do you see as you look around that inspires you to praise God?

....

....

....

....

....

....

Our loving God sees us and His attention is renewed each day; He never fails to rejoice in us.

> 'The faithful love of the LORD never ends! His mercies never cease. Great is his faithfulness; his mercies begin afresh each morning' (Lam. 3:22–23).

Create

Create a picture of what you have noticed today by drawing, using words, making a collage or any other medium.

Fearfully and wonderfully

'Thank you for making me so wonderfully complex! Your workmanship is marvellous— how well I know it.' **Psalm 139:14**

How well do we know ourselves? We read that we are 'fearfully and wonderfully made'. David also says that his 'soul knows it very well'. There is a sense of appreciation that shows a delight in the way God has made him. Our soul consists of our mind and heart, which can very easily play tricks on us if we happen to be in a low mood; or encourage us when we are more upbeat! Eleanor Roosevelt once said, 'Friendship with oneself is all important, because without it one cannot be friends with anyone else in the world.'

Let's take some time to check out some of the things that we know about ourselves, then we can begin to build a healthy relationship with ourselves!

Reflect and write

My favourite way to spend a day is...

....

....

....

Five things that make me smile are...

....

....

....

The words I'd like to live by are...

....

....

....

I couldn't imagine living without...

....

....

....

Three things that I do well are...

....

....

....

Three areas of my life where I would like to make improvements are...

....

....

....

Lord, help me to get to know and appreciate myself as You do. Thank You that You have created me fearfully and wonderfully. Thank You that You are (list five things that you appreciate about God):

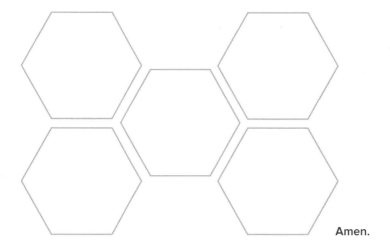

Amen.

Pause and consider...

'Dear friend, do what I tell you; treasure my careful instructions. Do what I say and you'll live well. My teaching is as precious as your eyesight—guard it! Write it out on the back of your hands; etch it on the chambers of your heart. Talk to Wisdom as to a sister. Treat Insight as your companion. They'll be with you to fend off the Temptress—that smooth-talking, honey-tongued Seductress.' **Proverbs 7:1–5,** *The Message*

When I go away for a few days I take a vanity case with me. It contains everything I need to get ready in the mornings including my hairdryer, make-up, shampoo and even cotton buds – it is invaluable to me. The day we moved house I left it behind, and when I realised, an hour into my journey, I immediately drove back to retrieve it; it is that important to me! (As well as being a thoughtful gift from my sister.)

Over these first seven sessions we have been considering our sense of identity and how verses in the Bible help us to develop the beauty within. But if we don't carry these verses with us, if we don't 'etch [them] on the chambers of [our] heart' we may not be affected positively by them. The writer of this chapter recognises the importance of storing these things in a place where they will make a difference.

On the Beauty Within weekend, we decorated small boxes and stored special mementoes in them. Beautiful boxes were created containing scriptures, items from the garden as well as personal reflections. One lady decorated only the inside of her box and kept the outside plain to show how special it was to work on her inner self – so creative.

As we explore what it means to have beauty within, as well as writing in this journal, maybe you could create an 'inner beauty box' and fill it with all the things that will inspire you to cultivate a 'gentle and quiet spirit' (1 Pet. 3:4). Alternatively, you could treat yourself to a beautiful notebook in which to collate verses and thoughts. You could be as creative as you like using crayons, felt-tip pens, pictures, torn images from magazines, washi tape, stencils, stickers, or ink stamps – anything that catches your imagination and helps to remind you that God notices *you*.

So far we have considered what it is to be known. How God know us, and how He wants us to know Him. God wants His name to be known by all humanity because He loves us all so much. Jesus said in John 17:24–26:

'Father, I want these whom you have given me to be with me where I am. Then they can all see the glory you gave me because you loved me before the world began! O righteous Father, the world doesn't know you, but I do; and these disciples know you sent me. I have revealed you to them, and I will continue to do so. Then your love for me will be in them, and I will be in them.'

In these verses we get a sense that being known by Him is as important as knowing of Him.

We also started to think about identity, and how our sense of identity begins in our inner being. What is tied up within your identity? Is it what others say about you, or your value as a friend, wife, mother or daughter? Does your career, life experiences, education and financial status have any influence? How we see ourselves can affect how we feel, behave and experience life.

Most importantly, how does God see us? He sees us as His daughters made in His image, and He delights in us. He knows we have things to sort out in our lives, and so He gently and lovingly guides us in ways in which we can grow and develop to reflect His image. *The Message* says to 'Cultivate inner beauty', so that with God's help we can be determined to transform some of the less than beautiful parts of us into areas of outstanding beauty! Let's embrace the fact that we are our Father's daughters. We bear His image. We are known and loved by Him. As you reflect on this, let it begin to transform your identity.

Dear Father God, as I journey with You through the pages of this journal, I pray that You will walk with me. I desire that Your presence will guide me into the truth that You delight in me. May that knowledge transform the beauty within, so I can experience the fullness of the abundant life You have promised. Amen.

I am made in God's image

'Yes, the Sovereign LORD is coming in power. He will rule with a powerful arm. See, he brings his reward with him as he comes. He will feed his flock like a shepherd. He will carry the lambs in his arms, holding them close to his heart. He will gently lead the mother sheep with their young.' Isaiah 40:10–11

Write

What is God like? Using different coloured pens, write as many characteristics of who He is as you can.

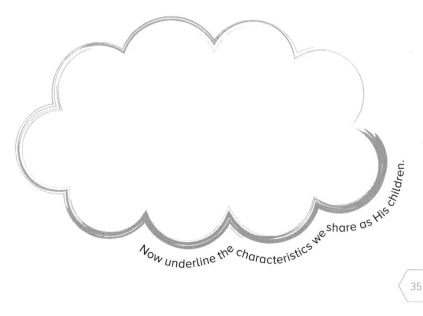

Now underline the characteristics we share as His children.

Isn't our creator God amazing? The Bible says that we share His characteristics. We might need to develop and grow these characteristics, but potentially we can reflect something of who He is as we spend time with Him and contemplate His nature. When we come into a relationship with the Lord, we are restored and there is nothing to stop us from becoming more like Him. As Pauls says:

> 'So all of us who have had that veil removed can see and reflect the glory of the Lord. And the Lord—who is the Spirit—makes us more and more like him as we are changed into his glorious image' (2 Cor. 3:18).

Jesus had a clear idea of who He was because of His close relationship with the Father and the Spirit. He described Himself as someone we could depend on and find life in. He is the good shepherd, the bread of life, He gives living water, and He releases us into freedom. Jesus didn't let others define Him – do we?

Write

What words would you use to describe yourself?

....

....

....

....

....

How do you think others see you?

....

....

....

....

....

How does God see you?

....

....

....

....

....

Reflect

Circle or highlight any statements that you have written that are biblically true. Hold on to the knowledge that, as a child of God, you are these things.

Loving God, help me to see myself as Your child.
May I develop and grow Your characteristics. Amen.

Restoring the image

'The Spirit of the LORD is upon me, for he has anointed me to bring Good News to the poor. He has sent me to proclaim that captives will be released, that the blind will see, that the oppressed will be set free...' **Luke 4:18**

Jesus recognised that many people were poor in spirit, held captive in some way, blind to what a relationship with God could be, and oppressed by circumstances and a skewed belief system. He came to set them, and us, free! We can so easily become trapped, imprisoned or brought low by how we see ourselves and how we view God, as well as by situations we are facing.

Jesus saw the need for restoration; for rebuilding something that needed fixing – our relationship with God. He demonstrated a clear and confident relationship with His Father that we can all have, and He did it with a conviction in who He was and why He was here. We have seen that God said He wants to make us like Him – in His image. We have also looked at ways in which we resemble the creator. So let's follow Jesus' example and embrace with confidence our wonderful relationship with God and who we are in Him.

Reflect and write

Are there areas of your character that need restoration? Prayerfully bring them before your loving Father and receive His healing. It can be helpful to write them down and release them into God's hands.

....

....

....

....

....

....

Meditate

Consider these precious words and let them dwell in your heart.

'For the LORD your God is living among you. He is a mighty savior. He will take delight in you with gladness. With his love, he will calm all your fears. He will rejoice over you with joyful songs' (Zeph. 3:17).

Write

Copy those restorative words from Zephaniah 3 and embellish them creatively. At the same time you could put on some worship music, and let your heart rejoice in who you are as a child of God who loves you, takes delight in you and sings over you. Let Him calm your fears and be your Saviour.

I am loved

'The goal is for all of them to become one heart and mind—Just as you, Father, are in me and I in you, So they might be one heart and mind with us. Then the world might believe that you, in fact, sent me. The same glory you gave me, I gave them, So they'll be as unified and together as we are—I in them and you in me. Then they'll be mature in this oneness, And give the godless world evidence That you've sent me and loved them In the same way you've loved me.' John 17:21–23, *The Message*

I have a beautiful new grandson, who has my unconditional love. He doesn't have to do anything to earn it – he has it! Who knew the strength of feeling that such a little person could generate? My heart is full of love for him. At such a young age, what he needs is lots of care and attention, to be fed, to be kept clean, to be held in loving arms, and to be spoken to gently and encouragingly. These are crucial needs to be met, not just optional conditions that would be good to have; without them there would be a deficit, not only in his care, but in his heart.

Similarly, we need to know we are loved in order to have a sense of security and belonging as individuals, and in our relationships with others. There is a lot of familial love in the verses in John 17, and an expression of a loving desire to see us experience the fullness of the Father's love for each one of us. How easy do we find it to accept this powerful love? Accepting it brings us to a place of security. We come to Jesus who is the fountain of life because His love never dries up or stops pouring out. We have a choice either to step into that love and bathe in it, or to live outside of it and experience a thirst.

Reflect and write

What does security and belonging mean to you?

Where do you seek it currently?

Jesus said, 'you've sent me and loved them In the same way you've loved me' (John 17:23, *The Message*).

Let that settle deep into your heart and thank God for His love.

Write a prayer or a few words to express what you feel about this kind of love.

....

....

....

....

....

Lavishly loved

'See what great love the Father has lavished on us, that we should be called children of God! And that is what we are!' **1 John 3:1, NIV**

Pondering on what it means to be loved by God is so important to understanding the beauty within each of us. When writing, I sometimes use a thesaurus to find alternative words to convey my meaning. For example, other words that mean 'lavished' are showered; inundated; heaped; deluged; poured. Try replacing the word 'lavished' in the verse above with one, or all, of these words, and see if it helps to add additional meaning to the verse.

Reflect

There are times when I can become prickly because I feel misunderstood. I ask God to bless me with His lavish love so I can respond in a more appropriate way. It is amazing how His love heals and enables us to feel more positive about ourselves. Spend some time allowing this truth to sink in and bless areas of your life where you may not feel particularly lovable. Remember God's love is unconditional and comes with lavish grace. 'He is so rich in kindness and grace that he purchased our freedom with the blood of his Son and forgave our sins. He has showered his kindness on us, along with all wisdom and understanding' (Eph. 1:7–8).

Reflect and write

Continue to reflect on how you are loved lavishly, excessively and generously. Express how you think and feel about this in words, pictures, or any other way that displays a heartfelt response.

I have an inheritance

'Furthermore, because we are united with Christ, we have received an inheritance from God, for he chose us in advance, and he makes everything work out according to his plan.' Ephesians 1:11

When you think of receiving an inheritance, what do you imagine? Some money? A property? Items of value? Whatever it is, an inheritance is something of sentimental or monetary value given to us by someone who loves and values us. It might even have the potential to make our lives a little easier.

The inheritance we have in Jesus outlasts any financial gain, and has immeasurable value for our inner beauty – the beauty that money cannot buy.

Reflect and write

I inherited from my dad his hair colour; some of his character traits and abilities; his love of singing and entertaining; and a few of his unique quirks of personality! What are some of the traits, interests, abilities you have inherited from parents or other special people in your life? Are there any you would like to improve or change? Write them over the word 'Me', embellishing the words describing traits you would like to improve, and crossing through the traits you would like to grow out of.

Below is a list of some of the things we receive as part of our inheritance in Jesus. Highlight the ones that have become part of your own life, and over the page feel free to write any others – remembering eternity begins now!

- Abundant life
- Eternal life
- Love and acceptance
- Sense of worth and purpose
- Power from God
- Righteousness
- Renewal and restoration
- Peace and hope

- Belonging
- Emotional health
- Transformation
- Renewed mind
- Fellowship
- Joy
- Sense of freedom

Looking at your list, is there anything that you feel you haven't yet fully embraced? Pray that God will bless you, and will reveal how to grow in that area and experience His healing.

'It is by his great mercy that we have been born again, because God raised Jesus Christ from the dead. Now we live with great expectation, and we have a priceless inheritance—an inheritance that is kept in heaven for you, pure and undefiled, beyond the reach of change and decay' (1 Pet. 1:3–4).

Cherished

'Praise the LORD, all you nations. Praise him, all you people of the earth. For his unfailing love for us is powerful; the LORD'S faithfulness endures forever. Praise the LORD!' **Psalm 117**

Cherishing others is something we do when we value and appreciate them. We hold them in high esteem and treasure their company and involvement in our lives.

Write

Who do you cherish and how do you show it?

....

....

....

....

Now write down how others cherish you.

....

....

....

....

Cherishing works both ways, doesn't it? We know God cherishes us, and we are going to spend a few days exploring how He does that, and what that does for our spirit. First, though, let's consider how we might cherish Him.

David is a good example of someone who articulated how he cherished God:

> 'Because of your unfailing love, I can enter your house; I will worship at your Temple with deepest awe' (Psa. 5:7).

> 'I bow before your holy Temple as I worship. I praise your name for your unfailing love and faithfulness; for your promises are backed by all the honour of your name' (Psa. 138:2).

Worship is an important means of showing our devotion to a loving heavenly Father, His precious saving Son and a very present Holy Spirit. But how else might we cherish Him?

Reflect and write

Prayerfully think through other ways in which you could cherish God. Write them in the space below.

Is God guiding you to any particular method?

Meditate

Spending time with God is precious in itself, not the means to something else. It is simply being with God and enjoying His presence.

Pause and consider...

'Understand, therefore, that the LORD your God is indeed God. He is the faithful God who keeps his covenant for a thousand generations and lavishes his unfailing love on those who love him and obey his commands.'
Deuteronomy 7:9

When God brought the Israelites out of slavery in Egypt, He was demonstrating His great power, and also His lavish love for His people. He promised them that He would be with them, and that they would inherit a land that would be fruitful. When Jesus left heaven to come and live among us, He also demonstrated great power and sacrificial love; and this was for the whole world so that everyone could experience and know the love of God.

Knowing this love is foundational for living a life where we don't have to strive to seek affirmation, attention, value or praise. It is a love that is poured out daily and is a fountain of life to us. It is a love we don't have to earn or perform for; we do not need to be perfect to receive it or enjoy it. It is a love that is unconditional, and encompasses all of us!

Having been involved in counselling and women's ministry for many years, I have heard so many women say that they find it difficult to receive love, or believe they are lovable. Tragically, unhappy relationships and low self-worth can make it difficult for some of us to accept that we can be loved, and so we either try to earn it by pleasing others, or protect ourselves by withdrawing from people. This hurts our inner being and leaves us with a deficit of love in our hearts.

Father God created us to be loved, so when we find it hard to receive it we experience pain. He longs to show His love abundantly and without hesitation. We know this because of what it says in John 3:16:

'This is how much God loved the world: He gave his Son, his one and only Son. And this is why: so that no one need be destroyed; by believing in him, anyone can have a whole and lasting life. God didn't go to all the trouble of sending his Son merely to point an accusing finger, telling the world how bad it was. He came to help, to put the world right again. Anyone who trusts in him is acquitted' *(The Message)*.

I believe there is a longing in God's heart to see each one of us restored and fully at ease with His love. He will help to put the broken pieces of our hearts back together, recreating the beauty within us. If this resonates with you and is your desire, let Him breathe His loving Spirit into you and restore, refresh and redeem your inner being. Remember – Jesus died for it.

'He was supreme in the beginning and—leading the resurrection parade—he is supreme in the end. From beginning to end he's there, towering far above everything, everyone. So spacious is he, so roomy, that everything of God finds its proper place in him without crowding. Not only that, but all the broken and dislocated pieces of the universe—people and things, animals and atoms—get properly fixed and fit together in vibrant harmonies, all because of his death, his blood that poured down from the cross' (Col. 1:18–20, *The Message*).

If you already celebrate and receive God's love, experience afresh the lavishness of it, the abundance of it, and worship the lover of your soul.

Imagine standing on a very firm foundation of love where you experience security and the knowledge that all is well. Feel the refreshing of the fountain of life pouring out His love, joy, peace, patience, goodness, kindness, faithfulness and gentleness into your heart. Sense your heart being filled up. Yes, we don't deserve it but He gives it anyway!

Let me encourage you to receive it, enjoy it, praise Him for it, worship Him and adore Him as we continue to consider the depth, breadth, width and height of this amazing, gracious love.

Precious Lord, You gave everything to show Your very great and lavish love for me. Help me to accept it and receive it into my heart. Guide me into that place of security, heal my soul, put the broken pieces back together and make me whole. You have the power – may I give You the glory. Amen.

I am chosen

'Since, then, you have been raised with Christ, set your hearts on things above, where Christ is, seated at the right hand of God. Set your minds on things above, not on earthly things. For you died, and your life is now hidden with Christ in God. When Christ, who is your life, appears, then you also will appear with him in glory.' **Colossians 3:1–4, NIV**

An amazing exchange takes place in our hearts because of what Jesus did for us on the cross. God paid a high price for sin to be defeated and we are the beneficiaries of His generosity. Because our new lives are 'hidden with Christ in God', our outlook and inner life is being renewed in the image of our creator; we are chosen and dearly loved; we can clothe ourselves with the characteristics of love that blesses others, and we can experience the healing 'peace of Christ' (v15).

Write

Read Colossians 3:1–17. Looking at verses 12 to 17, what are the characteristics of 'God's chosen people'?

All of these attributes will renew our inner beauty but some, like peace, may even be noticeable in our actions and on our faces! But it is important that we are proactive and play our part in receiving these characteristics. We are encouraged to 'set your hearts', 'put to death', 'clothe yourselves', 'put on love', 'let the peace', 'let the word', and finally, 'do it all in the name of the Lord Jesus'. Like the Colossians, we can get stuck in a rut. We need to let go of certain ways and embrace the new; the new is about knowing we are 'God's chosen people, holy and dearly loved'.

Reflect and write

Write below what difference it would make to yourself and others if you lived like 'God's chosen' person.

....

....

....

....

....

....

....

....

....

Dear God, help me to clothe myself every day with love that blesses others. Amen.

I am valued

'I pray that out of his glorious riches he may strengthen you with power through his Spirit in your inner being, so that Christ may dwell in your hearts through faith. And I pray that you, being rooted and established in love, may have power, together with all the Lord's holy people, to grasp how wide and long and high and deep is the love of Christ, and to know this love that surpasses knowledge—that you may be filled to the measure of all the fullness of God.' Ephesians 3:16–19, NIV

Are you able to comprehend the width, length, height and depth of Christ's love? To while away the time on long car journeys, my sister and I used to try to outdo one another in our declarations of love for our parents. It would include statements like, 'I love you as long as the longest road'! Our young, heartfelt assertions of love cannot even begin to compare to the dimensions of the love that Jesus has for each one of us. This kind of love develops a sense of value in us; the knowledge that we have a purpose in God's kingdom.

Why would Jesus have gone to all that trouble in leaving the glory of heaven and coming to earth if He didn't value us so much? He wants to strengthen our inner beings. It's helpful to remember that when we experience low self-esteem or face difficult issues.

Reflect and write

One way we can experience the 'power through his Spirit' in our inner being is when we face a situation where we don't feel personally equipped. In my early days teaching on CWR's Introduction to Biblical Care and Counselling course, I could have easily felt overwhelmed by the responsibility, but as I trusted in Him I certainly felt strengthened in my inner being by His power and enjoyed the process! How have you experienced this?

....

....

....

....

....

....

....

....

The awareness that we are valued, that God has a plan for our lives, builds into the beauty of our inner being. It brings a satisfaction and an appreciation that we were created for a purpose, and that strengthens us. Paul encourages us to put our roots down deep into this love so that we may be filled with 'all the fullness of God'. And why do we need this? Why do we need to be strengthened in our inner being? When we are fulfilling God's calling for our lives, we will probably be a target for the enemy to attack and pull us down. Fulfilling our purpose is a threat to Satan.

Not only are we known, but we need to know God deeply too. His power is at work within us, so let's embrace that truth as we seek to understand what He has called us to do. Proverbs 24:3–4 says, 'By wisdom a house is built, and through understanding it is established; through knowledge its rooms are filled with rare and beautiful treasures' (NIV). I hope you are beginning to understand that *you* are a beautiful treasure; *you* have value.

Reflect and write

What does it mean to you to be filled with 'all the fullness of God'?

I am free to be valued

'God is love. When we take up permanent residence in a life of love, we live in God and God lives in us. This way, love has the run of the house, becomes at home and mature in us, so that we're free of worry on Judgment Day—our standing in the world is identical with Christ's. There is no room in love for fear. Well-formed love banishes fear. Since fear is crippling, a fearful life—fear of death, fear of judgment—is one not yet fully formed in love.'
1 John 4:17–18, *The Message*

My wonderful tutor who walked alongside me through the CWR counselling course had a list of questions that referred to the concept of freedom. Each started with 'Am I free to...?'. Freedom within our minds and hearts is something to be prized. We can so easily be robbed of freedom by negative thinking and attitudes. When we read of the value God places on us, how free are we to receive it? Are we able to let His love have 'the run of the house'?

Reflect and write

Look at these questions below and answer them with either 'always', 'sometimes', 'rarely' or 'never'.

Am I free to make mistakes? _____

Am I free to love myself and others? _____

Am I free to forgive? _____

Am I free to change? _____

Am I free to succeed / fail? _____

Am I free to relax? _____

Am I free to say yes / no? _____

Am I free to receive from others? _____

Am I free to give to others? _____

Worry and fear are the enemies of freedom, and in 1 John 4 we are told that where there is love, there is no room for fear. When we are free to accept the love of God in our lives, we can walk in freedom. The New Living Translation puts it like this: 'If we are afraid, it is for fear of punishment, and this shows that we have not fully experienced his perfect love' (v18).

When we understand His perfect love for us, and we are able to love Him in return, it speaks of maturity. Those roots will have gone down deep, and we will truly know how much we are valued. Being valued to me means that I have worth, that my life counts for something, and that God rejoices that He made me!

Reflect and write

What does 'being valued' mean for you?

Prayerfully consider your answer to this question: 'Am I free to be valued by God and know my worth to Him?'

I have hope

'Hope deferred makes the heart sick, but a longing fulfilled is a tree of life.'
Proverbs 13:12, NIV

The amazing gift of life we have through Jesus is sometimes referred to as 'the divine exchange', where Father God has exchanged the life of His Son for us. What a privilege! Sometimes we don't live as though we have received that incredible gift; sometimes we let ourselves down and wonder if we have let God down too. I long to be a blessing to my heavenly Father and bring Him joy; when I feel that I do, my heart is filled with joy; when I feel that I don't, my heart is sick. Is this your experience too? Either way we are still loved!

There are many things I have hoped and prayed for; some have been realised and some have not. But if I put my hope in the desire to have those prayers answered in my own way and they are not, then my heart becomes 'sick'. My hope needs to be in God and His wisdom in these matters. We can encourage our hearts with the words of Isaiah 40:31: 'but those who trust in the LORD will find new strength' – and increase their inner beauty!

Reflect and write

Consider and write down some of the things that you have hoped for that have been realised. Let your heart rejoice in longings fulfilled.

Now write below those things you longed for but have not seen fulfilled. Ask God for inner peace, and allow the Lord to bring His presence into your heart and heal the emptiness you may be feeling.

As women we are life-givers. Even if we have never given birth, we bear the kind of fruit that can bring life to others in so many ways. What goes on in our inner being will produce fruit – fruit from our lips, our behaviour, our relationships and our intentions. The positive changes that take place in our hearts as we walk with God will produce good fruit. When we take seriously the words and life of Jesus, it will be like 'a life-giving fountain' (Prov. 13:14) for us. Looking at this chapter in Proverbs, we can see the value of wisdom, and a life based on that foundation produces beautiful things. What we reveal to others will often be a result of what's going on inside. Feeding on God's Word, times of worship, receiving His love, will all create that beautiful spirit we are seeking; and through our words and actions, Jesus will be revealed. How wonderful – and that's our hope, our tree of life.

Reflect, draw and write

On the page opposite, draw a tree with fruit on. Within the fruit, write ways where you are seeing fruit in your own life, for example, being more patient with close relatives.

I am alive!

'But God is so rich in mercy, and he loved us so much, that even though we were dead because of our sins, he gave us life when he raised Christ from the dead. (It is only by God's grace that you have been saved!) For he raised us from the dead along with Christ and seated us with him in the heavenly realms because we are united with Christ Jesus. So God can point to us in all future ages as examples of the incredible wealth of his grace and kindness toward us, as shown in all he has done for us who are united with Christ Jesus. God saved you by his grace when you believed. And you can't take credit for this; it is a gift from God. Salvation is not a reward for the good things we have done, so none of us can boast about it. For we are God's masterpiece. He has created us anew in Christ Jesus, so we can do the good things he planned for us long ago.' **Ephesians 2:4–10**

When Jesus found His disciples sleeping while supposed to be praying for Him, He declared, 'the spirit is willing, but the body is weak' (Matt. 26:41). Anybody who has attempted dieting or exercising might agree! For some, a toned and healthy body might be the ideal, but it requires a steadfast mind to accomplish it. We can understand Paul's dilemma when he says in Romans 7:15 'I don't really understand myself, for I want to do what is right, but I don't do it'. He was discussing the concept of struggling with sin.

There is often a fight going on inside us between our spirit and our flesh, or our renewed self and our old frail self. The beauty within belongs to the renewed spirit and true life. We are made alive, saved by grace, raised up, God's masterpiece, created in Christ. These are all life-giving, life-enhancing gifts from God. This new dimension we have been brought into literally bursts with life because it is the creator God who is the instigator.

Reflect

Read through the passage from Ephesians 2 again, as though it is written to you as an individual, eg, 'But God is so rich in mercy and he loved [me] so much...' What does that do for your heart and mind?

The truths contained in these verses can switch us on to the kind of living that connects us to the source of all life. Although we are living on earth and have earthly bodies, spiritually we can be attuned to something that will fill us with energy and excitement; and this energy source never loses its power.

Write

In the art world, what makes a 'masterpiece'? Write your thoughts within the frame.

Precious Lord, as I consider all You have done for me, and all that I am in You, I am overwhelmed. May the power of Your life-giving Spirit light up my life so that I might truly know I am alive in You. Amen.

Where do we live?

'Anna, a prophet, was also there in the Temple. She was the daughter of Phanuel from the tribe of Asher, and she was very old. Her husband died when they had been married only seven years. Then she lived as a widow to the age of eighty-four. She never left the Temple but stayed there day and night, worshiping God with fasting and prayer. She came along just as Simeon was talking with Mary and Joseph, and she began praising God. She talked about the child to everyone who had been waiting expectantly for God to rescue Jerusalem.' Luke 2:36–38

Anna positioned herself in a holy place where God chose to meet with His people. This was a sacred place, which declared God's presence and His authority. It was a visual dwelling and a sanctuary for people to worship. Her choice was to spend her days worshipping God and having fellowship with His people. Her devotion was deep.

What is our position? Where are we in relation to God's dwelling or indwelling? We have so many promises about our position in God through Jesus — how seriously do we take them? In the previous session, we read, 'For he raised us from the dead along with Christ and seated us with him in the heavenly realms because we are united with Christ Jesus' (Eph. 2:6). This has been a pivotal verse for me. As I ponder on it, my spirit is lifted and I recognise the privilege of my standing because of what Jesus did. Our walk is on this earth, but our spirit is united with Jesus and we can live in that perspective. That blesses every part of my being, and takes me deeper into His presence.

Anna was in the right place at the right time because of her dedicated, worshipping heart. We are in the right place because of Jesus' sacrifice.

Reflect

Spend time in God's presence – perhaps light a candle, listen to some worship music and reflect on your position in God. Here are some scriptures to help focus your attention.

'So now we can rejoice in our wonderful new relationship with God because our Lord Jesus Christ has made us friends of God' (Rom. 5:11).

'So just as sin ruled over all people and brought them to death, now God's wonderful grace rules instead, giving us right standing with God and resulting in eternal life through Jesus Christ our Lord' (Rom. 5:21).

'And since we are his children, we are his heirs. In fact, together with Christ we are heirs of God's glory' (Rom. 8:17).

'Yet now he has reconciled you to himself through the death of Christ in his physical body. As a result, he has brought you into his own presence, and you are holy and blameless as you stand before him without a single fault' (Col. 1:22).

Create

As you consider the verses above, creatively write thoughts or draw images that best convey where you see yourself in relation to where you are 'seated' or where you 'stand' in God.

A renewed life

'Now there was a Pharisee, a man named
Nicodemus who was a member of the Jewish
ruling council. He came to Jesus at night and
said, "Rabbi, we know that you are a teacher
who has come from God. For no one could
perform the signs you are doing if God were
not with him." Jesus replied, "Very truly I tell you,
no one can see the kingdom of God unless
they are born again." "How can someone be
born when they are old?" Nicodemus asked.
"Surely they cannot enter a second time into their
mother's womb to be born!" Jesus answered,
"Very truly I tell you, no one can enter the
kingdom of God unless they are born of water
and the Spirit. Flesh gives birth to flesh, but the
Spirit gives birth to spirit."' **John 3:1–6, NIV**

Upcycling is a current trend: taking something old,
refurbishing it to bring it up to date and give it a new
lease of life. Painstaking work is often involved in
this procedure. Nicodemus was an elderly man who wanted
to understand the ways of Jesus and was told that a renewing
process had to take place.

Reflect and write

Spend time reflecting on how you have come to know Jesus better over the years. What changes took place? How was your life renewed?

....

....

....

....

....

John's Gospel contains one of the most familiar verses in the Bible, but we cannot discuss the concept of an exchanged and cherished life without quoting it again: 'For God so loved the world that He gave His one and only Son, that whoever believes in Him shall not perish but have eternal life' (John 3:16, NIV). My husband, at the age of seven, heard this verse and gave his life to the Lord.

What does it mean to you?

....

....

....

....

....

....

Further on in John 3, Jesus talks about light and dark, good and evil, and God's mercy, grace and love.

No one is too old or too young, too good or too much a sinner to receive life in all its fullness. If you have opted for a 'beauty box', consider what you will include in it as you reflect on being chosen, valued, free, and having a renewed life. Let these devotions continue to create beauty within and transform your spirit and bring it life.

Precious Lord, You have done so much for me. Thank You for Your unconditional love that allows me to be enfolded in Your heart. You have enabled me to become part of Your family because Jesus died that I might live and live eternally. Help me to become more aware of what that means as I let it sink into my spirit. Amen.

Pause and consider...

Years ago, I went to an image consultant to discover which colours, as well as which shapes and styles of clothing, suited me best. It was fun, informative and I usually take the recommendations into consideration when buying clothes – but not always! We are all unique, there will be some colours and styles that enhance our natural complexions and shapes, and others that might make us look like the proverbial 'sack of potatoes'! Then, of course, there is the whole fashion scene that seems to want to put us into a mould of collecting the latest 'must-haves'. Does anyone else dislike that phrase?

I have confessed already to enjoying the process of dressing up and putting outfits together creatively. However, last year, I went on a buying clothes and shoes fast. It wasn't easy, but I coped. It meant that I had to become more creative and find new ways of wearing the clothes and shoes that were already in my wardrobe.

Our creator God has been very creative with us. Human beings are a variety of shapes and sizes, skin tones and personalities with varying gifts and abilities. I imagine He had the greatest delight in putting each of us together. Although He, in His wisdom, determined much of who we are, we have a part to play in the development of our personal growth and understanding. It is a gradual process as we become the person God intended us to be. Just like putting on new clothes, we can choose to put on God-given gifts. Paul says, 'So, chosen by God for this new life of love, dress in the wardrobe God picked out for you... And regardless of what else you put on, wear love. It's your basic, all-purpose garment. Never be without it' (Col. 3:12–14, *The Message*).

If our identity is caught up in the way we look, we might need to check up on which wardrobe of clothes we value most. God values the inner beauty, and so it is good to explore ways in which we can develop that further. Our inner beauty is often linked to our attitude and character. What is inside is often shown up when we face challenges, difficulties and hurts. In 1 Samuel 1, the story of Hannah reveals characters who exhibited human, but unhelpful, characteristics:

• Peninnah took pleasure in irritating Hannah;
• Elkanah failed to understand the distress his wife was facing, though he loved her dearly;
• Hannah was distraught at not being able to have children;
• Eli was insensitive towards Hannah and mistook her prayers for drunken ramblings.

It seems apparent that, along with her desire to have children, Hannah's sense of identity would be caught up with not being a mother. The depth of her feeling is evident in that she wept and could not even eat. The distress went deep and affected her inner being. Many of us will have felt a similar kind of longing and aching for something. There was an empty space in Hannah's life that she believed could only be filled by having a child. The longings we might feel are deeply held and eager to be satisfied. But Hannah came to pray because she understood that only God can bring complete satisfaction and wholeness.

Hannah prayed with an honest and compelling heart. God chose to answer her prayer by giving her a son who would become a major part in His purpose for the whole nation. His answer drew from her a song of praise and declaration of His greatness. When an emptiness within us becomes unbearable and we cry out to God, He will fill us and direct us towards His purpose, a purpose that will be valuable in His plan in our own lives and in His kingdom.

Because God created us, because we are made in His image, He knows how to fill us with what we need, and what we need is Jesus – He is our hope. Hannah knew God had answered her prayer, and she fulfilled her promise and purpose by yielding her son Samuel to live and grow in the Temple. Have you noticed where Samuel slept? 'Samuel was lying down in the temple of the Lord where the ark of God was' (1 Sam. 3:3, NIV). He was in the holiest of places; he was positioned in the right place to hear the voice of God calling clearly. We have talked about our position in God, and Samuel is another example of the importance of being in a good place. We may not live in a temple, but we are a temple of the Holy Spirit; 'Don't you know that you yourselves are God's temple and that God's Spirit lives among you?' (1 Cor. 3:16, NIV). It is as close as that for us. At any time, we can tune into God and His voice – what an amazing privilege! Being in this position keeps us connected, and able to live loved.

Looking again at Hannah's story, we see a lot of emotions displayed. We are emotional beings! Remembering we are made in God's image, emotions aren't feelings to be ignored or suppressed, but acknowledged and worked out. I have often heard people say, 'I shouldn't feel like that, it's wrong'.

Feelings are not wrong, they just are. It's what we do with them that counts; they are often an indication of what's going on inside. Peninnah was probably jealous of the attention Elkanah gave Hannah. Elkanah was most likely hurt that he wasn't enough for Hannah. Eli may have been disappointed by his sons' behaviour and took it out on Hannah.

God Himself is clearly an emotional being; He loves, feels pain, has compassion, becomes angered, is jealous for His children's love. Jesus wept for Lazarus, became angry in the Temple and was moved by the widow who lost her son. Emotions are God's idea. How we handle them is our responsibility. When I feel anxious, nervous, disappointed, irritated, embarrassed or sad, I ask myself three questions:

• What am I feeling?
• Why am I feeling it?
• What am I going to do about it?

Our loving Father created us with the ability to choose, and I can choose how to respond. My attitude and behaviour will either enhance my inner calm and beauty, or it will cause harm and lack of peace.

Hannah seemed to pour out her heart to God and graciously respond to an irritated Eli, who thought she was drunk:

'"Not so, my lord," Hannah replied, "I am a woman who is deeply troubled. I have not been drinking wine or beer; I was pouring out my soul to the LORD. Do not take your servant for a wicked woman; I have been praying here out of my great anguish and grief." Eli answered, "Go in peace, and may the God of Israel grant you what you have asked of him." She said, "May your servant find favour in your eyes." Then she went her way and ate something, and her face was no longer downcast' (1 Sam. 1:15–18, NIV).

This is a great study of someone who wasn't afraid of showing emotion but knew how to be courteous in the face of accusation, and she went away with a happy heart. This, indeed, is bearing good fruit. Galatians tells us that the fruit of the Spirit is love, joy, peace, patience, goodness, kindness, faithfulness, gentleness and self-control. Living a life that bears this fruit will reflect the image of God, bringing glory to Him.

As you pause and consider these thoughts, come before God like Hannah did and honestly:

- take up your position in Him, and experience the abundant life Jesus died to give you;
- take a look into God's face, and rejoice that He has chosen you as His beloved child;
- take a look at what you hope for, and let God fill any emptiness you might be experiencing;
- take a look at God's Word to see how much you are valued;
- take a look inside and discover how much of this truth penetrates your inner being.

Loving God, please bless me with your Spirit. Pour out Your love into my inner being so that you I will experience the truth that I am chosen, valued and dearly loved. Let the joy of the Lord by my strength, and may I stand knowing my position in You, and bring You praise as my roots go down deeper into You. Amen.

What's going on in my mind?

'Finally, be strong in the Lord and in his mighty power. Put on the full armour of God, so that you can take your stand against the devil's schemes. For our struggle is not against flesh and blood, but against the rulers, against the authorities, against the powers of this dark world and against the spiritual forces of evil in the heavenly realms. Therefore put on the full armour of God, so that when the day of evil comes, you may be able to stand your ground, and after you have done everything, to stand. Stand firm then, with the belt of truth buckled round your waist, with the breastplate of righteousness in place, and with your feet fitted with the readiness that comes from the gospel of peace. In addition to all this, take up the shield of faith, with which you can extinguish all the flaming arrows of the evil one. Take the helmet of salvation and the sword of the Spirit, which is the word of God.'
Ephesians 6:10–17, NIV

Most of us, at some time or other, have had troubling thoughts; ranging from a little concern through to deep anxiety or even panic. Each of us will have experienced a battle going on in our minds. It is in the mind that great ideas are won or lost, self-esteem is balanced or out of balance, belief is cultivated or damaged, peace is present or absent. Our minds have an enormous effect on our emotional, spiritual and even physical wellbeing. So, in terms of the beauty within, we need to explore the value of a beautiful mind.

Reflect and write

One area I battle with is that after sharing at a conference, I tend to go over what I have said and pull it to pieces! I am learning to let it go and leave it in God's hands, but there are times when my mind does battle with itself. What battles affecting your mind are you currently facing?

....

....

....

....

....

This passage from Ephesians 6 tells us that we are indeed in a battle and we need to recognise that the devil is out to win. One of the areas he intends to destroy is the mind, and unhelpful thoughts can be very destructive. The Holy Spirit on the other hand wants us to thrive. From Him we can expect comforting, uplifting thoughts that will enable us to experience clear, appropriate and balanced thinking – a far preferable option.

The part of the armour of God that refers to the mind is the helmet of salvation. The mind needs to be saved. When we become a Christian, we are saved and will live with Jesus forever, and that includes our minds and our thinking. The helmet is a great visual aid of protective armour to keep the mind safe. Helmets have been a vital part of armour over the centuries, with advancements in construction to combat the variety of ammunition as well as protecting the head from injuries caused by shock waves from explosions. Sometimes we can experience shock waves in life; the implications of which reverberate around our minds as we mull things over and over, until we feel drained from negative thinking.

Spend time reading those words in Ephesians again, and mentally putting on your armour, especially the helmet. What does each piece mean for you? Pray that as you do this, the Holy Spirit will walk with you and speak words of encouragement.

Capturing thoughts

'By the humility and gentleness of Christ, I
appeal to you – I, Paul, who am "timid" when
face to face with you, but "bold" towards you
when away! I beg you that when I come I
may not have to be as bold as I expect to be
towards some people who think that we live
by the standards of this world. For though
we live in the world, we do not wage war as
the world does. The weapons we fight with
are not the weapons of the world. On the
contrary, they have divine power to demolish
strongholds. We demolish arguments and
every pretension that sets itself up against the
knowledge of God, and we take captive every
thought to make it obedient to Christ.'

2 Corinthians 10:1–5, NIV

In the garden of our previous home, we had squirrels – cute!
Actually... not so cute. They enjoyed taking all the nuts
and fruit from our trees, which was OK, but they would
continually bury nuts in various parts of the garden and then,
later in the year, go round and dig them up. My lovely flower
pots were often taken apart as they searched for their hidden

feast. Apparently, to prevent other creatures stealing their stash, squirrels pretend to bury nuts in different locations, which results in even more damage. We tried to capture these little creatures in a humane trap and release them into a forest somewhere else, but to no avail!

In our own human strength we can feel powerless in trying to control unhelpful thoughts. They keep popping up when least expected and do damage all over again. Much of what we think can be negative, so it is a bit like trying to capture squirrels or moles without much success. So what can we do?

The Message puts verses 4 to 5 this way:

> 'We use our powerful God-tools for smashing warped philosophies, tearing down barriers erected against the truth of God, fitting every loose thought and emotion and impulse into the structure of life shaped by Christ. Our tools are ready at hand for clearing the ground of every obstruction and building lives of obedience into maturity.'

Fitting 'every loose thought and emotion and impulse into the structure of life shaped by Christ' reminds us that our minds need to line up with what Jesus says about us and to us. Earlier, we discussed the truth that we are cherished and loved unconditionally by God, and it is from that place that we can move forward in our thinking. Knowing the truth of His words, and being loved are essential weaponry against negative thought patterns.

Meditate

Let these words once again flood your mind and heart...

'And I pray that you, being rooted and established in love, may have power, together with all the Lord's holy people, to grasp how wide and long and high and deep is the love of Christ, and to know this love that surpasses knowledge – that you may be filled to the measure of all the fullness of God' (Eph. 3:17–19, NIV).

Reflect

Think about a pattern of negative thinking that you may be prone to...

• Where does that come from?
• How would you like to see that cycle of thinking changed?
• How can you bring that thought into the 'structure of life shaped by Christ'?

Write

What is on your mind now? Capture any negative thoughts by writing them down below, and then receive again the knowledge of God's great love as described in the verse opposite.

Heavenly Father, help me to be aware of, and capture, negative thinking. I pray that I may be rooted and established in Your love always. Amen.

Transformed mind

'Therefore, I urge you, brothers and sisters, in view of God's mercy, to offer your bodies as a living sacrifice, holy and pleasing to God – this is your true and proper worship. Do not conform to the pattern of this world, but be transformed by the renewing of your mind. Then you will be able to test and approve what God's will is – his good, pleasing and perfect will.' **Romans 12:1–2, NIV**

These verses have had a transformative effect on my life. After leading a group or speaking at a conference or teaching a course, I used to spend hours and even days going over in my mind the things I could have done better. Improving and developing material is one thing, but my mind was working in a way that created anxiety and discontent. It got to the point where it became like going down a dark tunnel of tangled thinking. I always came through and no permanent damage was done, but it was extremely uncomfortable and stomach churning.

The pattern I was conforming to was not godly or in the 'structure of life shaped by Christ' (2 Cor. 10:4–5, *The Message*). Reading that I could be transformed by the renewing of my mind, I had to believe it was possible – and believe it was possible for me.

The pattern of our thinking is often developed in childhood when we learn how to relate to the world around us, and what we believe the world thinks of us. I grew up in a positive atmosphere at home, but struggled to feel adequate in understanding some of the educative processes of my school life. My dominant thought was 'I'm not clever enough'.

Taking that thought and putting it into a structure was helpful and enabled me to work it through. The structure I used is the 'ABC theory' developed by Albert Ellis and taught in counselling training. The letters stand for:

A = activating event

B = belief you have cultivated

C = consequent emotion

For me, 'A' was not doing well in certain areas of education; 'B' was believing I wasn't clever enough; 'C' was experiencing anxiety over my ability to communicate to an adult audience. Self-awareness is key here, as it helps us find our way through when it comes to our thinking.

But we have to add a 'D' and an 'E' to this process:

D = dispute the lie

E = exchange it for the truth, which we find in Scripture

So again for me 'D' was saying I am clever enough to do what God has called me to in His name; and 'E' was a truth that equipped me to depend on Him such as:

> 'By his divine power, God has given [me] everything [I] need for living a godly life. [I] have received all of this by coming to know him, the one who called [me] to himself by means of his marvelous glory and excellence' (2 Pet. 1:3).

And:

> 'For I can do everything through Christ, who gives me strength' (Phil. 4:13).

Write

Next time you experience a pattern of negative thinking, I encourage you to think through and apply this structure:

A = activating event

....

....

....

B = belief you have cultivated

....

....

....

C = consequent emotions

....

....

....

D = dispute the lie

....

....

....

E = exchange for the truth, which we find in Scripture

....

....

....

Lord, I am sorry for believing this lie and living under it. Thank You that You created me with gifts and abilities that will bring glory to You. Thank You that You are the healer and that You will heal me from these debilitating thoughts. Transform my mind, dear Lord, I pray. Amen.

Focused thinking

'For this reason I remind you to fan into flame the gift of God, which is in you through the laying on of my hands. For the Spirit God gave us does not make us timid, but gives us power, love and self-discipline... What you have heard from me, keep as the pattern of sound teaching, with faith and love in Christ Jesus. Guard the good deposit that was entrusted to you – guard it with the help of the Holy Spirit who lives in us.' **2 Timothy 1:6–7,13–14, NIV**

Paul was both a mentor and an encourager for Timothy, and these letters were written to help equip him for leadership and to remind him that God would enable him to fulfil the work for which he was called. Timothy was young, but Paul encouraged him to focus on his gifts rather than his age when faced with difficult leadership situations. Age is not a prerequisite for leadership; we can be involved at some level whatever our age, young or old.

What other limitations do we put on ourselves in terms of ministry? We can be very good at talking ourselves out of being part of God's work because of feelings of inadequacy. Paul says, 'What you have heard from me, keep as the pattern of sound teaching'. Anxious thoughts render us helpless at times and, as already discussed, we need to create new positive patterns of thinking based on biblical truths.

Reflect

Read the scriptures below and let them create new patterns of thinking for you.

'Give all your worries and cares to God, for he cares about you' (1 Pet. 5:7).

'Jesus said to the people who believed in him, "You are truly my disciples if you remain faithful to my teachings. And you will know the truth, and the truth will set you free"' (John 8:31–32).

'For I am always aware of your unfailing love, and I have lived according to your truth' (Psa. 26:3).

'Think about the things of heaven, not the things of earth. For you died to this life, and your real life is hidden with Christ in God' (Col. 3:2–3).

'Train me, GOD, to walk straight; then I'll follow your true path. Put me together, one heart and mind; then, undivided, I'll worship in joyful fear' (Psa. 86:11, *The Message*).

'That is why I tell you not to worry about everyday life—whether you have enough food and drink, or enough clothes to wear... your heavenly Father already knows all your needs' (Matt. 6:25,32).

Write down some of the phrases and words that particularly fill your mind with positive thinking. Pray that the Holy Spirit will establish them in your heart.

Think on
these things

'And now, dear brothers and sisters, one final thing. Fix your thoughts on what is true, and honorable, and right, and pure, and lovely, and admirable. Think about things that are excellent and worthy of praise. Keep putting into practice all you learned and received from me—everything you heard from me and saw me doing. Then the God of peace will be with you.' **Philippians 4:8–9**

What do you find yourself thinking about? Apparently we have a tendency to think negatively more than we think positively – especially about ourselves. This scripture encourages us to focus on wonderful things, things that are clearly excellent. What a great idea! Holding on to negative thinking will only drag us down, this upbeat list of what to think about has the ability to lift us up.

Often, it is at night when we are trying to get to sleep that unhelpful thoughts can occur. This discourages sleep, which we need for optimum health. Practising the kind of thinking Paul urged the Philippians to adopt will help towards a healthy mind, and aid peaceful rest. He wrote this letter while under house arrest awaiting trial in Rome, so, undeniably, he understood the power of a sound mind in times of trouble.

Tucked away in Song of Songs is a little verse that describes exactly what happens when negative thoughts have the run of our minds: 'Catch all the foxes, those little foxes, before they ruin the vineyard of love, for the grapevines are blossoming' (Songs 2:15). Let's learn how to catch those 'foxes' so they stop ruining the garden of our minds and therefore our restfulness.

Reflect and write

Think about each of these types of thought that Paul mentions in Philippians 4 and write a few words to describe what they mean for you:

True:

....

....

....

Honourable:

....

....

....

Right:

....

....

....

Pure:

....

....

....

Lovely:

....

....

....

Admirable:

....

....

....

Excellent:

....

....

....

Worthy of praise:

....

....

....

Precious Lord, You have created so many wonderful things;
said some amazingly encouraging words to me; made an
incredible sacrifice to show me Your everlasting love and
have chosen to live in my life. Help me to rejoice in these
truths and focus my mind on these positive attributes. Amen.

Peace of mind

'Rejoice in the Lord always. I will say it again:
rejoice! Let your gentleness be evident to all.
The Lord is near. Do not be anxious about
anything, but in every situation, by prayer
and petition, with thanksgiving, present your
requests to God. And the peace of God, which
transcends all understanding, will guard
your hearts and your minds in Christ Jesus.'
Philippians 4:4–7, NIV

I really enjoy cooking and creating meals; the kitchen is a favourite room. In our home, I do all the planning, preparing and cooking and I am happy about that. Trying out new recipes is fun when I have the time and, these days, making them as healthy as possible is part of the challenge. This passage is a great recipe for peace, isn't it?

Ingredients:

• Rejoicing
• Gentleness
• No anxiety
• Prayer
• Petition
• Thanksgiving

Method:

1. You will need large quantities of rejoicing – you can always add to it.

2. Make gentleness a must for the success of this dish of peace.

3. Don't put in anxiety as it will sour the flavour – it isn't needed.

4. This dish requires prayer – put it in with a thankful heart.

5. You can add your petitions and requests and stir them in.

6. Put all these together and bring them to God who is at hand to help you with the mix.

7. You should end up with a healthy balanced meal of peace, which surpasses anything you will have tasted before. You will hardly believe it – it's so good!

The Bible encourages us to seek and pursue peace: 'Then keep your tongue from speaking evil and your lips from telling lies! Turn away from evil and do good. Search for peace, and work to maintain it. The eyes of the LORD watch over those who do right; his ears are open to their cries for help' (Psa. 34:13–15).

Although we have a part to play, Jesus knew how important peace would be to the beauty within, so He gave it as a gift. 'I am leaving you with a gift—peace of mind and heart. And the peace I give is a gift the world cannot give. So don't be troubled or afraid' (John 14:27). Jesus says that we cannot find this kind of peace anywhere but in Him, it is beyond the 'world's' ability to give us what we really need. And we really do need it, don't we?

Peace is a quality of mind and heart that is so precious our souls hunger for it.

Reflect and write

What does having peace of heart and mind mean for you? Write down some thoughts, and as you do, be prayerful and mindful of God's presence.

Thoughtfulness

'Love is patient and kind. Love is not jealous or
boastful or proud or rude. It does not demand
its own way. It is not irritable, and it keeps no
record of being wronged. It does not rejoice
about injustice but rejoices whenever the truth
wins out. Love never gives up, never loses
faith, is always hopeful, and endures through
every circumstance.' **1 Corinthians 13:4–7**

The most peaceful people I know are those who are
thoughtful. People who lovingly serve, bless and
encourage without expecting anything in return. These
words describe the attitude of such a person. As I read these
verses again, I am challenged by their honesty, humility,
openness, kindness and thoughtfulness. This is something to
be attained and practised, as the seeds of thoughtfulness are
grown in a heart of love.

Because Jesus has chosen to indwell us, we have love living
right inside us, and there should be no room for unlovely
behaviour – and yet... Well, there are times when we don't quite
live up to this beautiful picture of loving and living with others,
do we? Those times when the words just tumble out before we
check them; when niggles become frustrations and we use the,
'You make me...' phrases; when jealousy knocks on our minds

and we show resentment in some way. We don't always get this particular recipe right; those sour ingredients have a habit of sneaking in and ruining the perfect outcome.

Reflect and write

Think of someone who shows thoughtfulness. What do they do well? Which of those aspects would you like to develop? Write them down.

It is often in close relationships where we become aware of our less than loving attitudes. The verses in 1 Corinthians 13 are used in many marriage ceremonies as a foundation for a peaceful and loving home life. Living this way is a test for our independent spirit where, as Paul says, 'I don't really understand myself, for I want to do what is right, but I don't do it' (Rom. 7:15). This goes back to the battle we looked at: we want to be people who live this way, but, at times, we just don't seem to be able to pull it off!

Write

Create two lists:

1. Love is...	2. Love is not...

Tiredness, hormones, anxieties, time pressures and feelings of inadequacy can mar our decision to show more love, be kinder and more thoughtful. God knows all this about us, and we can run to Him for strength and an infilling of His presence.

Tell God about any struggle you might have in fulfilling this 1 Corinthians 13 kind of love. Honestly share your concerns with Him and pray through this passage with Him. Ask for His strength, His love, His compassion and His power to overcome any area you notice that needs developing within you.

Pause and consider...

What do you think of when we talk about peace? World peace; peace at home; peace in your own heart; peace between you and someone in your life; a peaceful place; being on your own for five minutes? We have spent a few sessions thinking about the beauty of peace in our own lives. We have recognised that the peace Jesus gives through the Holy Spirit is something that is deeper and more lasting. We are encouraged to pursue it.

The beauty of peace is something to attain and also something to give. Jesus said, 'Blessed are the peacemakers, for they will be called children of God' (Matt. 5:9, NIV). Peacemakers have been honoured by being awarded the Nobel Peace Prize, which is given 'to the person who shall have done the most or the best work for fraternity between nations, for the abolition or reduction of standing armies and for the holding and promotion of peace congresses.'* There have been a variety of groups and individuals who have worked tirelessly to bring about or promote peace within countries and people's lives. It is right that they are honoured.

In 1979, Mother Teresa was recognised as someone who was a peacemaker in the troubled lives of the poor, and was awarded for her humanitarian work. In her acceptance speech, she began with the prayer of St Francis of Assisi and then said:

'Let us all together thank God for this beautiful occasion where we can all together proclaim the joy of spreading peace, the joy of loving one another and the joy [of] acknowledging that the poorest of the poor are our brothers and sisters... God loved the world so much that he gave his son and he gave him to a virgin, the blessed virgin Mary, and she, the moment he came in her life, went in haste to give him to others. And what did she do then? She did the work of the handmaid, just so. Just spread that joy of loving to service. And Jesus Christ loved you and loved me and he gave his life for us, and as if that was not enough for him, he kept on saying: Love as I have loved you, as I love you now, and how do we have to love, to love in the giving. For he gave his life for us. And he keeps on giving, and he keeps on giving right here everywhere in our own lives and in the lives of others.'**

Each of us is called to be a peacemaker too; someone who serves from a heart of love. We may not influence a nation or a large people group, but we can affect and perhaps inspire those around us in the way we live our lives from a place of peace.

So what does a person who lives from a place of peace look like? James 3:17–18 says, 'But the wisdom from above is first of all pure. It is also peace loving, gentle at all times, and willing to yield to others. It is full of mercy and the fruit of good deeds. It shows no favoritism and is always sincere. And those who are peacemakers will plant seeds of peace and reap a harvest of righteousness.'

There is an inner contentment about a woman who is a wise peacemaker, someone who is at ease with herself and doesn't need to prove anything. She...

• doesn't want things only her way.
• doesn't turn away or withdraw.
• doesn't only give in for the sake of peace.
• doesn't just compromise.
• will stand alongside when you're hurting and share in the pain.
• will accept you for who you are today.
• will look for ways to encourage and see your strengths.
• will be out to do you good!
• will see you as a precious child of God.
• will have Christlike values and is in for the long-haul.

What a list of attributes! As I look at them I see someone who is peaceful to be with, and someone I would like to emulate. This is someone who is non-judgmental, and wants the best for the people she is in relationship with. Peacemakers are not peace keepers: they do not just give in, but create opportunities for peace to be worked through. And there is a reward for these people – no not the Nobel Peace Prize – they are called 'children of God'. A prize that is beyond earthly value, a heavenly prize worth receiving, and we can all prepare our acceptance speech for this one!

Being a child of God means we are heirs, and as such we are no longer slaves. In Romans 8:14–15 we read, 'For those who are led by the Spirit of God are the children of God. The Spirit you received does not make you slaves, so that you live in fear again; rather, the Spirit you received brought about your adoption to sonship. And by him we cry, "*Abba*, Father"' (NIV). Let's just spend time considering the difference between 'slaves' and 'sons'. As a child of God I experience unconditional love, and my confidence in that love does not depend on my performance; a slave believes love is linked to how well they perform. My position as a child of God is secure and if I fail, forgiveness and love are still forthcoming; a slave fears judgment and resentment builds. As a child of God I belong to a kingdom where I can operate in both priestly and kingly roles with grace because I am redeemed; a slave functions from a worldly perspective, and believes they are entitled to something due to performance.

Being a slave sounds like hard work with little or no peace; knowing I am a child of God, on the other hand, provides comfort and freedom of spirit, which promotes peace and wellbeing. This is why we can, in turn, offer peace to others in the way we choose to live and accept our place in God's kingdom. It is a firm foundation on which to stand and live from. Proverbs 4:23 says, 'Be careful how you think; your life is shaped by your thoughts' (GNB). Let's be careful how we think: do we see ourselves as children of God or slaves? Time and again Paul tell us to put off our old selves and put on the new. 'You were taught, with regard to your former way of life, to put off your old self, which is being corrupted by its deceitful desires; to be made new in the attitude of your minds; and to put on the new self, created to be like God in true righteousness and holiness' (Eph. 4:22–24, NIV). Therefore the attitude of our minds, accepting our place as a child of God, experiencing peace and the ability to be a peacemaker are all linked. The beauty within definitely promotes an outward beauty that in turn affects, blesses and inspires the lives of others.

As mentioned, Mother Teresa began her acceptance speech with the prayer of St Francis of Assisi, which is a good place on which to end these thoughts. Being a channel of God's peace comes from being at peace within our own minds because of knowing how much we are loved and accepted by a loving heavenly Father.

'Lord, make a channel of Thy peace that, where there is hatred, I may bring love; that where there is wrong, I may bring the spirit of forgiveness; that, where there is discord, I may bring harmony; that, where there is error, I may bring truth; that, where there is doubt, I may bring faith; that, where there is despair, I may bring hope; that, where there are shadows, I may bring light; that, where there is sadness, I may bring joy. Lord, grant that I may seek rather to comfort than to be comforted, to understand than to be understood; to love than to be loved; for it is by forgetting self that one finds; it is forgiving that one is forgiven; it is by dying that one awakens to eternal life.' **St Francis of Assisi**

*Alfred Nobel, quoted on nobelpeaceprize.org
[accessed October 2018]

**Mother Teresa – Acceptance speech, taken from nobelprize.org
[accessed October 2018]

God blesses

'Samuel did what the LORD said. When he arrived at
Bethlehem, the elders of the town trembled when they
met him. They asked, "Do you come in peace?" Samuel
replied, "Yes, in peace; I have come to sacrifice to the
LORD. Consecrate yourselves and come to the sacrifice
with me." Then he consecrated Jesse and his sons and
invited them to the sacrifice. When they arrived, Samuel
saw Eliab and thought, "Surely the LORD's anointed
stands here before the LORD." But the LORD said to
Samuel, "Do not consider his appearance or his height, for
I have rejected him. The LORD does not look at the things
people look at. People look at the outward appearance,
but the LORD looks at the heart."' **1 Samuel 16:4–7, NIV**

Samuel knew the blessing of the Lord on his life. He was
a man set apart as a prophet, and all of Israel came
to recognise it (1 Sam. 3:19–20). Initially, even he was
drawn in by the physical appearance of Jesse's son Eliab, but
God said something that revealed an aspect of His character:
He isn't influenced by what a man looks like, but is interested
in his heart. This, of course, goes for us as women too. In an
age where outward beauty is celebrated as something to be
attained, we can so easily be swayed by what we see at first
glance. What really counts in God's kingdom is the beauty of
the character within, which is something that is revealed as we
spend time with one another.

Samuel was left in no doubt as to God's choice. He had to wait until the very last son was introduced – young David. 'Then the LORD said, "Rise and anoint him; this is the one." So Samuel took the horn of oil and anointed him in the presence of his brothers, and from that day on the Spirit of the LORD came powerfully upon David' (1 Sam. 16:12–13, NIV). It was after this encounter with Samuel that he battled the enemy and killed Goliath, while letting the whole nation know how he felt about the power of God.

If ever a man revealed what was going on in his inner being, David did. Reading the Psalms shows us the powerful emotions David felt, the deep love he had for God and the expressions of mourning he experienced in times of trouble and shame. David understood something of the character of God, and he reflected that in his own life. Paul spoke about this in Pisidian Antioch when he unfolded the history of Israel, and said that God saw David as a man after His own heart.

Reflect and write

In what ways are David and God's heart similar?

....

....

....

....

....

....

....

What makes an impression on you when you meet others for the first time?

....

....

....

....

....

....

....

Now we know David was not perfect: he made some choices with devastating consequences, yet God blessed him. None of us is perfect either, and yet God chooses to bless us too. David honoured Saul but dishonoured Uriah, Bathsheba's husband. He wrote psalms of passionate praise and others of passionate agony. We are complex beings who fluctuate between good days and bad days.

Pray that you will be conscious of God's blessing on your own life and give Him praise.

God releases

'Show me the right path, O LORD; point out the road for me to follow. Lead me by your truth and teach me, for you are the God who saves me. All day long I put my hope in you. Remember, O LORD, your compassion and unfailing love, which you have shown from long ages past. Do not remember the rebellious sins of my youth. Remember me in the light of your unfailing love, for you are merciful, O LORD.' **Psalm 25:4–7**

All of us have stories to tell; we are women with a history that is unique to us. We have all had both wonderful and painful experiences that make us who we are today. In neglecting or disregarding those times in our lives, we may not appreciate the profound ways they have shaped us. Many of God's people didn't always have it easy, life was not continuously glorious. Ruth, Esther, Joseph, among others, faced difficult times, but they allowed those encounters to shape them into courageous and influential people – they were history makers.

Reflect and create

Consider some of the incidents in your own life that have been pivotal for you. Create a timeline with high points and low points to illustrate those experiences.

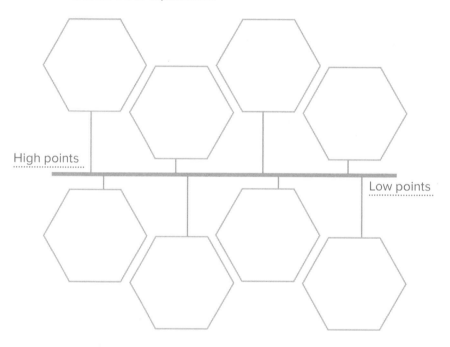

High points

Low points

Difficult times can produce the characteristic of perseverance. James 1:12 says, 'God blesses those who patiently endure testing and temptation. Afterward they will receive the crown of life that God has promised to those who love him.' God clearly walks with us through the joys and sorrows of life. The book of James describes the ways in which such times help to form us – for example, David is aware of his shortcomings and longs for God to lead and guide him, teaching him how to live righteously.

Looking back over our personal history will reveal some things we are not proud of. This was true for David and he asked God not to remember them. We have a Father who is forgiving, who releases us from things of the past that would seek to hold us back. These can be sins, memories, relationships and behaviours. Jesus came to bring freedom to our souls and release us into all that He has for us –'the crown of life'. Our history is part of our lives, we cannot rub it out or deny it; but we don't need to let it hold us back. History informs us, it is not for nothing.

As you consider your life journey so far, write out Psalm 25:4–7 in your own words and, as you pray it, let God's Holy Spirit heal and release you from some of those hurts, and show you how they have helped you to mature.

....

....

....

....

....

....

....

....

....

Saving grace

'Then he turned to the woman and said to Simon, "Look at this woman kneeling here. When I entered your home, you didn't offer me water to wash the dust from my feet, but she has washed them with her tears and wiped them with her hair. You didn't greet me with a kiss, but from the time I first came in, she has not stopped kissing my feet. You neglected the courtesy of olive oil to anoint my head... "I tell you, her sins—and they are many—have been forgiven, so she has shown me much love. But a person who is forgiven little shows only little love." Then Jesus said to the woman, "Your sins are forgiven." The men at the table said among themselves, "Who is this man that he goes around forgiving sins?" And Jesus said to the woman, "Your faith has saved you; go in peace."' **Luke 7:44–50**

This story is a wonderful snapshot of how Jesus loves – He cherishes. This woman had lived a sinful life and had come to realise that Jesus was the one she needed in order to find peace for her soul. She didn't allow circumstances or the situation to stop her following her heart. Often, what can prevent us from fully receiving God's love is our belief that we're not good enough. And Jesus clearly shows us that this way of thinking is not valid in God's kingdom. He publicly cherished her for her adoration. He lovingly embraced her act of humility, and released her from the effect of her sin.

Isn't Jesus wonderful here? He is our champion, and we can come to Him with our souls bared and receive His peace. I imagine she must have felt cleansed deep inside. This cleansing, this cherishing is available for us too; all we have to do is come before Jesus and let Him restore us. The key is to be self-aware and know what's going on within ourselves, to not let circumstances fester and make us sour, to bring our brokenness to Him in humility and allow Him to heal us and reveal the beauty within.

Reflect and write

Read the story in full (Luke 7:36–50), and consider each of the characters.

What characteristics did Jesus show?

....

....

....

....

What characteristics did the Pharisees show?

....

....

....

....

What do you think the woman was feeling when she entered the Pharisee's home?

....

....

....

....

How do you think she felt when she left?

....

....

....

....

Thank You for cherishing me, Lord. Your love gives me the freedom to come to You and open my soul. Your saving grace releases me from fear and heals my heart. You are my champion! Amen.

God forgives

'Meanwhile, Saul was uttering threats with every breath and was eager to kill the Lord's followers. So he went to the high priest. He requested letters addressed to the synagogues in Damascus, asking for their cooperation in the arrest of any followers of the Way he found there. He wanted to bring them—both men and women—back to Jerusalem in chains. As he was approaching Damascus on this mission, a light from heaven suddenly shone down around him. He fell to the ground and heard a voice saying to him, "Saul! Saul! Why are you persecuting me?" "Who are you, lord?" Saul asked. And the voice replied, "I am Jesus, the one you are persecuting! Now get up and go into the city, and you will be told what you must do."... Ananias went and found Saul. He laid his hands on him and said, "Brother Saul, the Lord Jesus, who appeared to you on the road, has sent me so that you might regain your sight and be filled with the Holy Spirit." Instantly something like scales fell from Saul's eyes, and he regained his sight. Then he got up and was baptized. Afterward he ate some food and regained his strength.' **Acts 9:1–6,17–19**

U p to this point, Saul had persecuted the Christian community known as 'The Way'. He was fanatical about destroying the Early Church. But God had other plans for this zealous man! I imagine He looked at Saul's character and personality, and saw the potential for the kingdom. Jesus was also a passionate man and He felt strongly about His Church, so it was as if Saul was persecuting Him. The rest, as they say, is history. Saul went on to become Paul, the most incredibly devoted servant and apostle of Christ.

Reflect and write

What are you passionate about?

You might imagine that Saul's actions would be unforgivable, but not for our loving Father. His heart is always to forgive. The message for us, as we explore discovering the beauty within is that we need to receive God's forgiveness, and we need to forgive others – our inner life depends on it. The importance of forgiveness to God is demonstrated on the cross; it is crucial to renewal, refreshing and restoration. Forgiving others is not letting them off the hook, but taking the hook out of ourselves.

'Test me, LORD, and try me, examine my heart and my mind; for I have always been mindful of your unfailing love and have lived in reliance on your faithfulness' (Psa. 26:2–3, NIV).

Paul was as zealous in this new life as he had been in his old life, but the focus of his attention had changed. The leadership skills and charisma hadn't altered, these were needed for the work he was to do. He also used his history to demonstrate the mercy and power of God.

What is God revealing to you?

....

....

....

....

....

....

....

Let the scales fall from your eyes, and let Him pour out His grace and mercy over you.

Forgiveness

'Therefore, as God's chosen people, holy
and dearly loved, clothe yourselves with
compassion, kindness, humility, gentleness and
patience. Bear with each other and forgive one
another if any of you has a grievance against
someone. Forgive as the Lord forgave you.
And over all these virtues put on love, which
binds them all together in perfect unity. Let
the peace of Christ rule in your hearts, since
as members of one body you were called to
peace. And be thankful.'
Colossians 3:12–15, NIV

We come back to this wonderful passage again, and focus on the aspect of forgiveness. In a conversation Jesus had with Peter in Matthew 18, He told him that forgiveness was an ongoing quality needed within our relationships, and He illustrated it with a directive parable about an unforgiving servant. This powerfully portrayed the heart of God towards us, and His desire for us to have the same heart towards others.

But it's not easy, is it? When we have been deeply hurt, humiliated, damaged, maligned and even abused by someone, we can feel justified in holding on to resentment and unforgiveness. We may say, 'Why should I let them off the hook?'

Memories, subsequent behaviours and beliefs about ourselves can be the result of some of these acts of unkindness, which have the potential of keeping us locked up in a place of pain. But we really do not have to remain there. We have a way through as we look at these words from Paul; ways that will encourage us to be set free from hurt and pain.

Reflect

Read this section's passage again and highlight meaningful words and phrases.

The first stage of moving towards forgiveness is knowing this, we are *all* forgiven. We said previously that this is crucial to renewal, refreshing and restoration – vital to the beauty within. We are told here that we are 'chosen people', 'holy', 'dearly loved', we have the 'peace of Christ' since we are 'called to peace'.

We need to remember that we are not called to be the judge and jury of the lives of others; that is God's remit!

> 'Now all has been heard; here is the conclusion of the matter: fear God and keep his commandments, for this is the duty of all mankind. For God will bring every deed into judgment, including every hidden thing, whether it is good or evil' (Eccl. 12:13–14, NIV).

Reflect and pray

Taking your time, work through these steps with your loving Father.

1. Praise God for His loving forgiveness towards you, and receive it.

2. Is there a secret resentment, unforgiveness or pain in your heart? Bring it to God in prayer and decide you want to let it go.

3. Acknowledge your feelings and tell God about them.

4. Reflect on the event or events causing you pain without judgment, and tell the Lord your thoughts.

5. Be willing to reconcile these things in your own heart by letting the Holy Spirit heal the pain.

6. Hand the judgment over to God, let Him deal with the 'secret thing'. (It may help to go through these steps with a very trusted counsellor / friend / prayer partner.)

7. Walk free!

Lord, I pray that Your peace will be the controlling factor in my life; not pain or hurt. Help me to decide daily to walk with You, receiving the inner calm of Your Holy Spirit to release me from holding on to those things that would destroy that peace. Amen.

Life and peace

'So now there is no condemnation for those who belong to Christ Jesus. And because you belong to him, the power of the life-giving Spirit has freed you from the power of sin that leads to death. The law of Moses was unable to save us because of the weakness of our sinful nature. So God did what the law could not do. He sent his own Son in a body like the bodies we sinners have. And in that body God declared an end to sin's control over us by giving his Son as a sacrifice for our sins. He did this so that the just requirement of the law would be fully satisfied for us, who no longer follow our sinful nature but instead follow the Spirit. Those who are dominated by the sinful nature think about sinful things, but those who are controlled by the Holy Spirit think about things that please the Spirit. So letting your sinful nature control your mind leads to death. But letting the Spirit control your mind leads to life and peace... And Christ lives within you, so even though your body will die because of sin, the Spirit gives you life because you have been made right with God.' **Romans 8:1–6,10**

Paul clearly had to triumph over inner obstacles such as guilt and regret that may have been set up because of his past history, and we will need to overcome some of ours too. Reading what he says about life in the Spirit, it seems as if this is something particularly dear to his heart. Paul talks about the struggle the mind has between following earthly desires and godly desires; and the battle is won or lost in in our human spirit.

Our spiritual self was brought to life when we set our hearts on Jesus and He filled us with His Spirit. The Holy Spirit is completely involved in our everyday lives, with our everyday challenges, decisions and activities. He is able to equip us with everything we need to deal with the trials in our minds.

Reflect and write

As we read what Paul says about living by the Spirit, write down your reflections on the following aspects:

We are not condemned (v1).

....

....

....

....

We are set free (v2).

....

....

....

....

There is an end to sin's control over us (v3).

....

....

....

....

Controlled by the Spirit, our thoughts please Him (v5).

....

....

....

....

We have life and peace (v6).

....

....

....

....

Our spirit is alive (v10).

....

....

....

The mind can cause such a lot of trouble for us, but we are encouraged to be aware of the power of the Spirit in us so that we don't have to succumb to the 'sinful nature'. When we co-operate with the Spirit of God and let Him fill our inner being, then He will help us, guide us and strengthen us towards a fantastic freedom. For 'the law of the Spirit who gives life has set you free'. And that is truly beautiful.

Take time to pray to, and praise, God for His gift of life to you. Ask that the Spirit will lead you into this life of freedom in your inner being.

> Dear Lord, thank You for the Spirit of life. Precious Lord, fill me with Your Spirit that I may know the freedom of life in the Spirit. Amen.

Heart flow

'My child, pay attention to what I say. Listen carefully to my words. Don't lose sight of them. Let them penetrate deep into your heart, for they bring life to those who find them, and healing to their whole body. Guard your heart above all else, for it determines the course of your life. Avoid all perverse talk; stay away from corrupt speech. Look straight ahead, and fix your eyes on what lies before you. Mark out a straight path for your feet; stay on the safe path. Don't get sidetracked; keep your feet from following evil.' **Proverbs 4:20–27**

My husband is an avid photographer and enjoys taking photos of water in its various states, but particularly waterfalls. We might trek miles for that all-important shot. Sometimes the source provides a trickle and sometimes an overflow that roars – they can be awe-inspiring!

What goes on in us will determine what comes out from us; becoming more aware of God's part in that by His Spirit will result in an overflow. Guarding the heart speaks of protecting it, which does not mean putting up a wall that no one can penetrate! Rather it means nurturing it by feeding on truth, speaking life, fixing our attention on righteous living, treading the path God has for us. If we do this our hearts will 'determine the course of our lives'. Or, as other Bible translations put it: 'everything you do flows from it' (NIV); 'that's where life starts' (*The Message*); 'For from it flow the springs of life' (AMC).

Reflect and write

What does it mean for you to guard your heart?

We have seen that God blesses, releases, cherishes, forgives, lives in us, renews and transforms. What a magnificent Father we have. He wants to nurture us with His loving kindness, wisdom and understanding into women who are made in His image, know we are cherished, forgiven, walk in freedom and have renewed thinking. That sounds like a recipe for living exceptionally from a place that is the 'unfading beauty of a quiet and gentle spirit' (1 Pet. 3:4). Let these thoughts settle in your heart, mind and spirit.

Find an inspiring image of a waterfall online or remember one that you have visited in the past. Let it inspire you to pray. Draw or write your prayer with illustrations.

Pause and consider...

I recall being on a weekend away with people from my church. We stayed in a good hotel with comfortable rooms, a sea view, great food and fun-filled activities. There was encouraging and thought-provoking teaching, which inspired us to move forward as a body of God's people into thinking about our effect and place in our local community. But being on a weekend together, away from the pressures of time and duties, gave us many opportunities to share our stories and get to know one another on a deeper level.

Stories are really important; revealing our experiences, thoughts and feelings about them tell others something about who we are. For me, this was the really valuable part of the weekend. Hearing the joys and sorrows of life within family, the workplace, our journeys with God, church life and personal thoughts and feelings, give insight to where we are on the voyage of life.

Our own stories are part of our equipment as we listen and encourage others; we can grow through our experiences, and use them to enable us to share life with others on a deeper level. Jesus came to earth as a man, and grew in wisdom as He learned about humanity from personal understanding. As we go through different situations, we can also grow in compassion and genuine empathy for others facing similar life challenges.

One of my own profound life experiences was being unable to have children. It became central to my emotions and thinking in my twenties and early thirties. I went through a regular grieving process, but kept in contact with my loving heavenly Father so that it didn't stop me from functioning in my relationships and work life. This part of my story has become a source of connection with others who have experienced loss, and perhaps a feeling of emptiness in their lives, as well as those going through difficulty in having a family of their own. It sent me to the source of life time and again, and helped me to learn to depend on Him for my sense of worth and purpose.

One lesson I learnt early on was that I am complete in Him. I once had to give a talk at a women's group entitled 'Being Complete'. Initially I wasn't too keen on the idea as I didn't *feel* particularly complete! But the study gave me an understanding that, though there was pain in the lack, I wasn't 'less than' because of it. I could encourage others to know that truth also. One lady felt able to say, 'I'm leaving this group today feeling that I can walk tall like I haven't for a long time!'

For my husband and I, we chose to go down the road of adoption after reading:

'Sing to God, sing in praise of his name, extol him who rides on the clouds; rejoice before him – his name is the LORD. A father to the fatherless, a defender of widows, is God in his holy dwelling. God sets the lonely in families, he leads out the prisoners with singing; but the rebellious live in a sun-scorched land' (Psa. 68:4–6, NIV).

What a wonderful choice we made! We have two fabulous children, a son-in-law and now a beautiful grandson who is our joy and delight. But those years are still part of our story, the pain is still part of our memory, the empathy we feel is still part of our equipping. We wanted to make sense of that experience, so it became part of a beautiful tapestry portraying a life lived with God rather than an episode we pushed aside and resented.

So pause and consider what experiences you have had that might be part of your 'beauty box' of equipment to use? Is it time to see them in a new light?

There are, of course, parts of our story that we may need to learn to let go of in terms of the negative effect they have on us. We have looked at the positive power of forgiveness, and the freeing aspect of releasing people to God. As part of CWR's counselling model, we encourage clients to explore their history in order to discover ungodly patterns of behaviour, which may have started at certain significant times in their lives. For me, it was a bullying experience at school, and the subsequent fear of making close friendships just in case I got hurt. This was a debilitating behaviour that caused loneliness, jealousy and feelings of inferiority. The problem with living like this is the thing you are afraid of is often the thing you most long for.

Recognising the strong hold this difficult time had over me, I was able to make a choice to cut off those negative strings by: a) understanding what the impact was; b) forgiving the teenagers who behaved badly; c) praying for forgiveness for my own subsequent behaviour and d) letting God's love pour in and fill those years of sadness. He enables us to overcome, through Him we become conquerors!

'Who will bring any charge against those whom God has chosen? It is God who justifies. Who then is the one who condemns? No one. Christ Jesus who died — more than that, who was raised to life — is at the right hand of God and is also interceding for us. Who shall separate us from the love of Christ? Shall trouble or hardship or persecution or famine or nakedness or danger or sword? As it is written: "For your sake we face death all day long; we are considered as sheep to be slaughtered." No, in all these things we are more than conquerors through him who loved us. For I am convinced that neither death nor life, neither angels nor demons, neither the present nor the future, nor any powers, neither height nor depth, nor anything else in all creation, will be able to separate us from the love of God that is in Christ Jesus our Lord' (Rom. 8:33–39, NIV).

Beauty grows through understanding and expressing the various parts of our story as we interact with both God and others. There is such joy in relationships where we can be honest. I have to say that, for me, those relationships need to feel safe before I am able to share some parts of my story and the emotions that go along with them!

Remembering that we are vulnerable, often our tales are told through tears, and God sees our tears. Tears are a release, and we need not be embarrassed when they come, either for ourselves or for others. They can lead to a time of comfort. Being involved in pastoring people who weep when they tell their stories is a privilege; letting the tears appear is important, we don't need to stop them. God has provided us with this outlet and even stores them. David knew this in times of conflict with the Philistines: 'You keep track of all my sorrows. You have collected all my tears in your bottle. You have recorded each one in your book' (Psa. 56:8).

And in Revelation we are told that:

'I heard a voice thunder from the Throne: "Look! Look! God has moved into the neighborhood, making his home with men and women! They're his people, he's their God. He'll wipe every tear from their eyes. Death is gone for good—tears gone, crying gone, pain gone—all the first order of things gone." The Enthroned continued, "Look! I'm making everything new. Write it all down—each word dependable and accurate"' (Rev. 21:3–4, *The Message*).

What a wonderful message of hope. And we must not lose hope, for we have an eternal hope:

'That is why we never give up. Though our bodies are dying, our spirits are being renewed every day. For our present troubles are small and won't last very long. Yet they produce for us a glory that vastly outweighs them and will last forever! So we don't look at the troubles we can see now; rather, we fix our gaze on things that cannot be seen. For the things we see now will soon be gone, but the things we cannot see will last forever' (2 Cor. 4:16–18).

What mirror are we looking in for a glimpse of beauty? The reflection looking back at us can be disappointing if all we see is our negative past, the effects of destructive relationships, loss and rejection. We need to look up into the face of our redeemer who reflects a vision of blessing, release, love, forgiveness, wholeness and comfort. The more we look at Him the more we will reflect His glory and exude His pleasing aroma.

'In the Messiah, in Christ, God leads us from place to place in one perpetual victory parade. Through us, he brings knowledge of Christ. Everywhere we go, people breathe in the exquisite fragrance. Because of Christ, we give off a sweet scent rising to God, which is recognized by those on the way of salvation—an aroma redolent with life' (2 Cor. 2:14–16, *The Message*).

Lord God, thank You that Your strong arms can enfold me in a place of safety. May my past be part of the rich tapestry of my story as I share my life with others. May my experiences never become a stronghold that debilitates my journey in You. Let me be a sweet fragrance bringing the knowledge of Jesus wherever I go. Amen.

Jesus and His Father

'Jesus answered, "I am the way and the truth and the life. No one comes to the Father except through me. If you really know me, you will know my Father as well. From now on, you do know him and have seen him." Philip said, "Lord, show us the Father and that will be enough for us." Jesus answered: "Don't you know me, Philip, even after I have been among you such a long time? Anyone who has seen me has seen the Father. How can you say, 'Show us the Father'? Don't you believe that I am in the Father, and that the Father is in me? The words I say to you I do not speak on my own authority. Rather, it is the Father, living in me, who is doing his work."' **John 14:6–10, NIV**

I f you are a parent, you would probably like to know that when your child visits another family they would behave in a way that would make you feel proud. You invest in their life journey, hope they fulfil their potential, and experience satisfaction making the most of the opportunities that come their way. God showed Himself to be a proud Father when He said, 'You are my Son, whom I love; with you I am well pleased' (Mark 1:11, NIV).

Jesus is confident in His relationship with His Father to the point that He knows that His disciples see God through Him. Father and Son were, and are, intimately involved with each other's lives. Because of this, Jesus was completely at ease with who He was; He knew where He had come from and knew where He was going. This love bond created within Him a confidence that enabled Him to live undefended and open hearted, to teach with authority, to challenge a lack of integrity in leaders, and love His disciples and friends unconditionally.

Write

Consider the attribute of 'confidence'. How would you define it?

....

....

....

....

....

....

Reflect and write

How confident do you feel in your relationship with God? Would you like to increase it? In what way? Use the cloud opposite to write your thoughts.

God's love for us is as powerful and complete as it was for His Son, and so we too can have the kind of confidence that Jesus had, but often we don't. Sometimes we find it difficult to trust and believe in God's all-encompassing love for us, so we defend ourselves, and we don't always feel at ease in our inner being. Yet it is in our inner being that God chooses to dwell by His Holy Spirit. We are containers of the presence of God. Now that *really* creates beauty within us!

Let what Jesus says about the Holy Spirit being in us (John 14:17) breathe life into your soul. Let Him lead you to a place of greater confidence in who you are in God, and to a life lived more assuredly.

Right at the beginning of this journal, we talked about the fact that we could have a two-way conversation with the Lord. Jesus had many times when He conversed with His Father. Take time to speak to God, and to listen to what He is saying to you.

Write

What would you like to say to God?

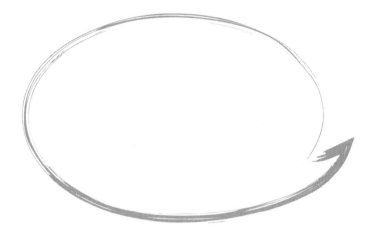

What is He saying to you?

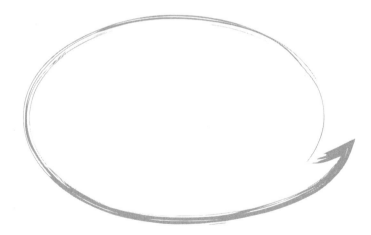

Spend time reading those words of Jesus in John 14 again and receive them as a direct truth right into your heart.

Jesus changes us

'Jesus entered Jericho and was passing through. A man was there by the name of Zacchaeus; he was a chief tax collector and was wealthy. He wanted to see who Jesus was, but because he was short he could not see over the crowd. So he ran ahead and climbed a sycamore-fig tree to see him, since Jesus was coming that way. When Jesus reached the spot, he looked up and said to him, "Zacchaeus, come down immediately. I must stay at your house today." So he came down at once and welcomed him gladly. All the people saw this and began to mutter, "He has gone to be the guest of a sinner." But Zacchaeus stood up and said to the Lord, "Look, Lord! Here and now I give half of my possessions to the poor, and if I have cheated anybody out of anything, I will pay back four times the amount." Jesus said to him, "Today salvation has come to this house, because this man, too, is a son of Abraham. For the Son of Man came to seek and to save the lost."' **Luke 19:1–10, NIV**

Using the Russian dolls on page 20 as a visual aid again, we see it reflects what goes on inside of us in terms of awareness. We have different layers, and each layer represents a new awakening to the transforming power of Jesus' love. As He gets deeper into our spirit, we become more like Him. It can take time, and for many of us some of those layers can be painful to open up.

Zacchaeus was a chief tax collector, a man despised and named a 'sinner', but he was curious about Jesus and wanted to see Him. The feeling was mutual! Jesus had a desire to meet with Zacchaeus also, and invited Himself to his house; and this is where an amazing miracle took place right in the centre of Zacchaeus' heart. It was as if Jesus' presence bypassed the layers and got straight to the inner part of his being and a change took place.

As the people around began to mutter their disapproval, Zacchaeus 'stood up' and declared his change of heart by being willing to restore what he had taken from others with four times the amount. I believe he allowed the presence of Jesus to penetrate the ugly parts of his life and restore them to a beautiful and generous spirit.

Write

What layers do you observe in Zacchaeus' life?

....

....

....

....

....

What emotions, beliefs and behaviours might you attribute to him?

....

....

....

....

....

What changed?

....

....

....

....

....

Jesus' presence can do that for our layers too. If, like Zacchaeus, we 'want to see who Jesus is', then His presence can transform each area that needs healing and make them whole. Take time to invite Jesus into an area of your life that needs changing, and as you 'see' Him, let the healing begin.

> Thank You, dear Lord, that You have a transforming presence. As I spend time there, change me so that I become more like You. Amen.

Jesus and relationships

'As Jesus and the disciples continued on their way to Jerusalem, they came to a certain village where a woman named Martha welcomed him into her home. Her sister, Mary, sat at the Lord's feet, listening to what he taught. But Martha was distracted by the big dinner she was preparing. She came to Jesus and said, "Lord, doesn't it seem unfair to you that my sister just sits here while I do all the work? Tell her to come and help me." But the Lord said to her, "My dear Martha, you are worried and upset over all these details! There is only one thing worth being concerned about. Mary has discovered it, and it will not be taken away from her."' **Luke 10:38–42**

Just take a moment to consider the different relationships you have from family through to friends and colleagues. There are so many, aren't there? We have many areas of influence within those relationships and also varying levels of intimacy.

Reflect and write

Write your name in the centre of the diagram below and the names of others in the appropriate hexagon. Highlight those who support and encourage you. Underline the name of any person that you need to invest more time in order to develop the relationship. What is the balance? Add other social circles or work groups if needed.

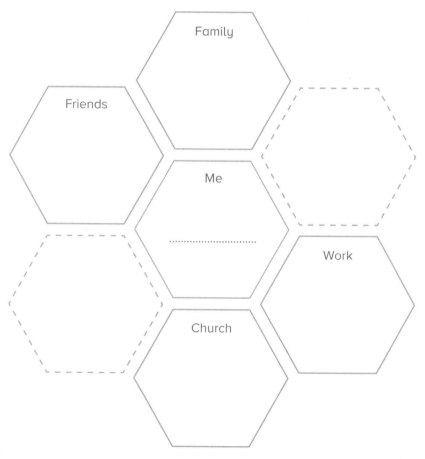

We probably behave differently in some, if not all, of those connections because each of us is unique with varying personalities and needs. God created us because He wanted relationship with us as a loving Father. Jesus spent time with friends because He enjoyed their company, and wanted to spend significant time with them. It was obvious that many people longed to be with Him; they followed Him wherever He went, and hung on His every word — He was a great friend.

Ecclesiastes 4:10 says, 'If one person falls, the other can reach out and help. But someone who falls alone is in real trouble.'

Friendship is worth investing in, both to give and to receive. Francois de La Rochefoucauld said, 'A true friend is the most precious of all possessions and the one we take least thought about acquiring.' Within our relationships there can be times of tension as here with Martha and Mary. However, later, in the account of their brother's death and coming to life, we see them lovingly supporting one another (John 11). Martha and Mary began to understand the importance of serving with their strengths instead of comparing with one another, and we need to do that in our relationships too. Appreciating the abilities in others frees us to be who we are with our own strengths.

It is important for our wellbeing to invest in relationships that will encourage us and spark the best in us. Part of our growth and development will be dependent on those connections. Part of nurturing that gentle spirit will involve people who love and support us.

Reflect and write

Look at the diagram of names again. Prayerfully reflect on ways you can encourage and bless the people in your life. Are there some changes you might need to make?

....

....

....

....

....

....

Lord, thank You for the people in my life. I want to be a good friend to others and support them. Help me to be aware of those who love and support me and want to bless me. Amen.

Jesus and the Holy Spirit

'If you love me, keep my commands. And I will ask the Father, and he will give you another advocate to help you and be with you for ever – the Spirit of truth. The world cannot accept him, because it neither sees him nor knows him. But you know him, for he lives with you and will be in you. I will not leave you as orphans; I will come to you... All this I have spoken while still with you. But the Advocate, the Holy Spirit, whom the Father will send in my name, will teach you all things and will remind you of everything I have said to you. Peace I leave with you; my peace I give you. I do not give to you as the world gives. Do not let your hearts be troubled and do not be afraid.' **John 14:15–18,25–27, NIV**

Whenever people we love come to visit and the time comes for them to leave, afterwards there is often a period that feels empty, quiet and perhaps even lonely. I have often wondered if, when Jesus left the disciples, they felt such a strong void it was painful. Jesus knew it was coming and, as a loving friend, began to prepare them for it. Nonetheless, their focus for three exciting and productive years was apparently lost. But Jesus knew something they could not possibly know, they would be so filled with His Spirit that it would be as if He were living right there inside them, guiding them.

The intimacy that Jesus describes here is something that can bring delight to every part of us. It can feed our minds, encourage our hearts and satisfy our spirits.

Reflect and write

As we absorb what Jesus says about the Spirit, write down your reflections on the following aspects:

'be with you for ever' (v15)

....

....

'lives with you and will be in you' (v17)

....

....

'will teach you all things' (v26)

....

....

'will remind you of everything I have said' (v26)

....

....

Jesus promises that intimacy will also be with Him and the Father: 'I am in my Father, and you are in me, and I am in you' (John 14:20, NIV). The bottom line for what we are like inside is: when Jesus lives within us – He is the beauty. We just need to recognise it, and let Him take His place on the throne of our hearts.

This intimacy with Jesus is something He wants us to receive and develop so His beauty can penetrate our very being, and help us become more like Him. We need to pause here and enjoy what Jesus is offering once again.

Reflect and create

Find a quiet place, perhaps light a candle, and enjoy the wonder and beauty of Jesus. Write, draw or creatively record your thoughts on the opposite page.

Jesus and me

'Are you tired? Worn out? Burned out on religion? Come to me. Get away with me and you'll recover your life. I'll show you how to take a real rest. Walk with me and work with me—watch how I do it. Learn the unforced rhythms of grace. I won't lay anything heavy or ill-fitting on you. Keep company with me and you'll learn to live freely and lightly.'
Matthew 11:28–30, *The Message*

This is a favourite version of this text with many people I know. It gives a clear picture of the fact that Jesus knows us and our needs so well, and wants to be involved in our everyday lives.

As women, we can often feel tired with the varying responsibilities we carry. Tick the way(s) you most regularly handle your responsibilities. Do you:

⬡ let them overwhelm you?
⬡ let them stack up?
⬡ handle them one at a time?
⬡ plan and prepare?
⬡ do things last minute and love the challenge?

We are all different and deal with things in our life differently. Look at the methods you ticked. Is there anything you would like to change?

In Matthew, Jesus says He wants to help us carry our roles, and to teach us how to live more efficiently. Don't we all want to find 'real rest' and 'the unforced rhythms of grace'? Rest is an important part of nurturing ourselves; how do you take it? God made it clear that we should enjoy a rest when He gave us the Ten Commandments; and He Himself rested after creating the heavens and the earth.

I have a friend who, when feeling overwhelmed by too many activities (she doesn't like saying 'No'!), writes them all down on sticky notes and places them out in front of her. She will pray over them and then start thinning them out. What a brilliant idea! It is certainly one I have chosen to adopt.

Reflect and write

Get some sticky notes and write down each of the things that take your time and effort — one for each note. Where are the priorities? Is there anything you need to let go of? Write your thoughts down here.

....

....

....

....

What Jesus is saying here is not just about making us feel good; it is so very important to understand that Jesus' desire for us to come to Him is based on a future hope and glory that Paul talks about in Romans 5:1–2:

'Therefore, since we have been justified through faith, we have peace with God through our Lord Jesus Christ, through whom we have gained access by faith into this grace in which we now stand. And we boast in the hope of the glory of God' (NIV).

We have 'peace with God through our Lord Jesus Christ' and 'gained access by faith into this grace'. His peace, His grace, His rest – let these bless you today as you come to Him. He will give us every opportunity to develop these qualities and He also provides the resources to accomplish it. How wonderful!

Loving Lord Jesus, I pray that I will learn to trust You for my rest. Teach me how to live freely and lightly and stand on Your promises to me. Amen.

Created to worship

'Keep me safe, my God, for in you I take refuge. I say to the LORD, "You are my Lord; apart from you I have no good thing." I say of the holy people who are in the land, "They are the noble ones in whom is all my delight." Those who run after other gods will suffer more and more. I will not pour out libations of blood to such gods or take up their names on my lips. LORD, you alone are my portion and my cup; you make my lot secure. The boundary lines have fallen for me in pleasant places; surely I have a delightful inheritance. I will praise the LORD, who counsels me; even at night my heart instructs me. I keep my eyes always on the LORD. With him at my right hand, I will not be shaken. Therefore my heart is glad and my tongue rejoices; my body also will rest secure, because you will not abandon me to the realm of the dead, nor will you let your faithful one see decay. You make known to me the path of life; you will fill me with joy in your presence, with eternal pleasures at your right hand.' **Psalm 16, NIV**

Reading this psalm, two aspects stand out: firstly, David felt secure in a place of refuge, and secondly he was compelled to worship the Lord. This is a wonderful psalm, which points to a wonderful God who provides a place of security where we can discover true beauty.

Contained within Psalm 16 are so many reasons to worship God:

• He keeps me safe;
• He's my refuge;
• He makes my life secure;
• I have a delightful inheritance;
• I will not be shaken;
• my body rests secure;
• He will not abandon me;
• He shows me the way my life should go;
• He fills me with joy;
• He fills me with eternal pleasures.

How amazing!

Highlight the reasons in the list above that particularly encourage your heart to worship at the moment. Praise God as you do.

Our worship glorifies God and puts Him in the highest place; it keeps Him before us and helps us focus on the source of our lives. It is an act of obedience and pleases Him; it is an act of adoration and yet it also lifts our spirits and breathes life into us too. Worship is something we can do alone, in small groups or in a large congregation. It can be quiet and meditative or loud and praiseworthy. Worship engages our whole being and blesses our whole being as we see in this psalm.

We were created to worship God, and He is eager to receive our worship. Jesus underlined a command to love God for who He is; 'Love the Lord your God with all your heart and with all your soul and with all your mind and with all your strength' (Mark 12:30, NIV). Part of loving God is to worship Him and tell Him how wonderful He is, not just with your words but with all of your being.

Reflect and write

What style of worship do you enjoy? What aspects of the Father, Son and Holy Spirit compel you to worship?

Precious Lord, I worship You, I adore You and I glorify Your name. You are truly wonderful. You are magnificent and holy, and You are kind and merciful. You are worthy. Amen.

Women of worth

'A wife of noble character who can find? She is worth far more than rubies... She selects wool and flax and works with eager hands. She is like the merchant ships, bringing her food from afar. She gets up while it is still night; she provides food for her family and portions for her female servants. She considers a field and buys it; out of her earnings she plants a vineyard. She sets about her work vigorously; her arms are strong for her tasks. She sees that her trading is profitable, and her lamp does not go out at night... When it snows, she has no fear for her household; for all of them are clothed in scarlet. She makes coverings for her bed; she is clothed in fine linen and purple... Charm is deceptive, and beauty is fleeting; but a woman who fears the LORD is to be praised.' **Proverbs 31:10,13–18,21–22,30, NIV**

If you made a list of all that you accomplish in a week it would make impressive reading. Women are known for their ability to multitask, having their minds on more than one thing at a time. Let's face it – we are very capable beings! The Proverbs 31 woman is often one who is maligned for being too perfect with far too many achievements; and yet, if we look closely, she can be seen as a fruitful woman who uses her skills to bless, encourage and experience fulfilment in her everyday life.

If you compare your list of weekly tasks with her list, you will see that you share many, if not all, of the same duties. We buy food (v14), plan for and prepare meals for family and friends (v15), go to work or work at home (v16), have to make ends meet (v18), volunteer in the community or at church (v20), and buy or make clothes for the family and ourselves (vv21–24). And because we are unique in our personalities, we will each come to these tasks in our own way. She brings good to those in her life, which is something we aspire to do also.

Write

Make a list of the things you spend time doing throughout the week.

How can you approach them in a new way?

The key to this woman's life is found in verse 30: 'a woman who fears the LORD is to be praised'. Knowing the love of the Father, recognising that, in Him, 'we live and move and have our being' (Acts 17:28, NIV), can enable us to live fulfilled lives. We may not be involved in as many things as we read here, but if our heart is in what we do – as hers is – we will experience a real sense of satisfaction. And we will be fruitful. Here we see a mature attitude towards everyday life where 'Whatever you do, do well' (Eccl. 9:10).

Dear Father, help me to appreciate the things I'm involved in and to try to do them well so I might be a blessing to others and glorify You. Amen.

Clothed
with strength

'She is clothed with strength and dignity; she can laugh at the days to come. She speaks with wisdom, and faithful instruction is on her tongue. She watches over the affairs of her household and does not eat the bread of idleness. Her children arise and call her blessed; her husband also, and he praises her: "Many women do noble things, but you surpass them all." Charm is deceptive, and beauty is fleeting; but a woman who fears the LORD is to be praised. Honour her for all that her hands have done, and let her works bring her praise at the city gate.' **Proverbs 31:25–31, NIV**

I have always been attracted to people who conduct themselves with dignity. They have an inner strength that enables them to respond rather than react to life's experiences. They may not say they have it 'all together', but they seem to handle challenges in a measured way. They are people of strength rather than strong people who might dominate or try to control. Their attributes are that they take care to listen attentively, relate with an open mind and heart, enjoy seeing others achieve, become aware of any changes they need to make within their own attitudes and walk humbly. They also let God take the lead!

Reflect and write

What, for you, are the characteristics of 'dignity'?

....

....

....

....

Which of those characteristics would you most like to see develop within yourself?

....

....

....

....

Women of dignity have a healthy sense of self-respect, a poise and beauty that goes beyond skin deep. Of course, this woman is reflecting a picture of wisdom, as much of Proverbs does, and as a wise woman, she is not trying to be perfect but is depending on her perfect Father. If we long to be dignified, have inner strength, have no fear of the future, speak with wisdom, instruct kindly and be watchful with diligence, then we too need to depend on our perfect heavenly Father who will give us all we need to live wisely.

Living wisely is about having a mature attitude, and maturity is achieved over time. Life's experiences, both positive and negative, teach us how to 'do life'. Growing in character is part of the maturing process alongside learning from one another. This kind of maturity is truly beautiful.

Reflect and write

Consider the qualities of wisdom. Which are important to you?

Loving Father, thank You that You want me to move towards maturity. Enable me to walk with dignity and have inner strength in You. Develop the beauty within me as I learn to trust in and depend on You. Amen.

Pause and consider...

Beauty within is a wonderful subject to consider. I have enjoyed exploring it and seeing where it has taken me. I hope that you have found this spiritual journey an encouragement to your inner being. But I'm also aware that there is still much to learn about achieving that inner peace. There are times when life and people challenge my peace and dignity, and in those times I pray for wisdom.

Even after spending time reflecting on the woman in Proverbs 31, my thoughts still manage to turn to the busy day ahead and how to achieve it all. Does that sound familiar? We have enough hours in the day to accomplish all that God asks of us. If we are overloaded it is because we have probably picked up too much responsibility! Again, does that sound familiar?

I started my own personal journal by writing: 'The day ahead – in fact the week – isn't something I am laughing at. The pressure is on. Time is not the only element – there is also energy and strength! Help!'

Then I remembered the promise in Isaiah 40:28–31:

'Do you not know? Have you not heard? The LORD is the everlasting God, the Creator of the ends of the earth. He will not grow tired or weary, and his understanding no one can fathom. He gives strength to the weary and increases the power of the weak. Even youths grow tired and weary, and young men stumble and fall; but those who hope in the LORD will renew their strength. They will soar on wings like eagles; they will run and not grow weary, they will walk and not be faint' (NIV).

I copied these verses into my journal as it always seems to have more impact. Then I prayed: 'Lord, clothe me with strength and dignity and increase my power to complete the work in the days ahead. As I look to and hope in You, renew my energy, help me to soar, run and walk through these days with joy and laughter in my heart.'

As I write, I am having a good day; I don't feel under any pressure right now and my heart is wonderfully joyful. We need to keep the powerful promises of God before us, such as what He said in Isaiah 55:10–11:

'The rain and snow come down from the heavens and stay on the ground to water the earth. They cause the grain to grow, producing seed for the farmer and bread for the hungry. It is the same with my word. I send it out, and it always produces fruit. It will accomplish all I want it to, and it will prosper everywhere I send it.'

Apparently, the words 'And God said...' appear over two thousand times in the Bible. He has so much to say to us; He wants to communicate His heart to us. To read God's Word is to be exposed to life-giving truth and we can't fully understand Him without it.

Psalm 119:1 declares we will be blessed and walk righteously if we read and obey the Word of God. It also says:

'I have tried hard to find you—don't let me wander from your commands. I have hidden your word in my heart, that I might not sin against you' (Psa. 119:10–11).

The purity of a diamond determines its value; and in Psalm 119:9 we read that a young person can keep pure by living according to His Word, so we need to know what the Bible says.

In our busy lives, we don't always give time to reading and meditating on Scripture, and yet we know that if we do, our lives are enriched. So how do we come to spending time reading the Bible? It has been suggested that a pattern may include:

• coming to the Word prayerfully;
• reading a portion of scripture;
• thinking about that scripture in detail;
• trying to understand the times and people it was written for;
• applying the scripture personally.

Some read and then meditate without any agenda and let the words sink in. I tend to picture the biblical scene and imagine what it must have been like in that situation; then consider what the Spirit might be saying to me by asking God to reveal His truth.

Whichever method we use, the Word will be part of that changing process as we let it become hidden in our hearts. All the scriptures we have read during this spiritual journey have encouraged us to understand the blessing of God's love, and knowing that can bring fruitfulness to our lives. We have been challenged by considering the part our mind plays in how confident we feel about His love for us, as well as how it affects what we think of ourselves.

If this is something you have struggled with, I pray that you are coming into a place of thankfulness for His wonderful, life-giving love. Being thankful is good for our souls. Having a gratitude list is therapeutic and lifts the spirit as well as the face! As we noted at the beginning, laughter lines are preferable to frowning ones.

One of the first things we teach our children is how to say 'Thank you'. Its polite! I can remember a friend waiting patiently at the front door while her little boy refused to say thank you for spending the day with us – it seemed to take a long time for him to respond! How quickly do we respond to God's goodness, I wonder? And it is about wonder, isn't it? If we truly consider God's greatness and majesty in comparison with our weakness and deficiencies, it leaves us in a place of wonder that He loves us so much.

What are you thankful for? For family and friends; health and happiness; a home and a job? There are so many things that we do have, and yet there are times when we tend to focus on what we don't have. Thankfulness creates in us a real sense of peace and joy. Being thankful literally feeds a positive outlook on life and a sweeter inner being. We will actually be better people to live with! It doesn't mean we can't challenge difficulties, or become sad when life is not good; that would be unreal. But there may be times, without good reason, when we fall into the temptation of being less than thankful.

It's at times like this I try to lift my eyes up and look at the wonder of God the Father, the Son and the Holy Spirit and let that take me to a place of thankfulness.

Speak or sing out Psalm 100 with me:

'Shout with joy to the LORD, all the earth! Worship the LORD with gladness. Come before him, singing with joy. Acknowledge that the LORD is God! He made us, and we are his. We are his people, the sheep of his pasture. Enter his gates with thanksgiving; go into his courts with praise. Give thanks to him and praise his name. For the LORD is good. His unfailing love continues forever, and his faithfulness continues to each generation.'

I pray, Lord, that Your life will be in me so that my inner life will grow in beauty. I want to glorify You in all that I do. Thank You for who You are and all that You do. Amen.

Notes

Inspiring
Women

Two ways to spend quality time with God

Inspiring Women Every Day

Written by women for women, these daily Bible reading notes offer insights that can be applied to your life every day. Discover more titles in the Inspiring Women range on our website.

Courses and Seminars

Our courses and seminars are designed for women of all ages and walks of life, creating opportunities to dig deeper into a relationship with God. Come and enjoy insightful teaching, worship and warm fellowship.

We can also bring some of our courses to your church or small group.

Find out more about all our resources and courses for women at
cwr.org.uk/inspiringwomen

Devotional Journals by Jen Baker

If you enjoyed this book, you might like these other journals, which explore more key themes. Each journal includes scriptures and thought-provoking questions.

God is good.
He has good plans for you.

Fear and regrets can often hold us back. Learn how to overcome such challenges by exploring different 'Freedom from' themes and delve into a transformative time with God.
ISBN: 978-1-85345-917-7

God's love for us is limitless...

He wants us to live a life full of purpose, unrestricted by the things that try to lessen our true identity in Jesus.
ISBN: 978-1-78259-398-0

Learn how to think like the child of God that you are!

What we believe affects every area of our lives. So how can we meditate on God's Word until His truth becomes our belief?
ISBN: 978-1-78259-754-4

Courses and seminars

Waverley Abbey College

Publishing and media

Conference facilities

Transforming lives

CWR's vision is to enable people to experience personal transformation through applying God's Word to their lives and relationships.

Our Bible-based training and resources help people around the world to:
• Grow in their walk with God
• Understand and apply Scripture to their lives
• Resource themselves and their church
• Develop pastoral care and counselling skills
• Train for leadership
• Strengthen relationships, marriage and family life and much more.

Our insightful writers provide daily Bible reading notes and other resources for all ages, and our experienced course designers and presenters have gained an international reputation for excellence and effectiveness.

Our venue, Waverley Abbey House, provides excellent facilities in idyllic settings – ideal for both learning and spiritual refreshment.

CWR Applying God's Word
to everyday life and relationships

CWR, Waverley Abbey House,
Waverley Lane, Farnham,
Surrey GU9 8EP, UK

Telephone: **+44 (0)1252 784700**
Email: **info@cwr.org.uk**
Website: **cwr.org.uk**

Registered Charity No. 294387
Company Registration No. 1990308